Rosie John
Doesn't Live Here Any More

One Family's Journey In Eldercare

by
Tom Begert-Clark

Bloomington, IN   authorHOUSE™   Milton Keynes, UK

AuthorHouse™
1663 Liberty Drive, Suite 200
Bloomington, IN 47403
www.authorhouse.com
Phone: 1-800-839-8640

AuthorHouse™ UK Ltd.
500 Avebury Boulevard
Central Milton Keynes, MK9 2BE
www.authorhouse.co.uk
Phone: 08001974150

*In the interest of privacy and to ensure anonymity in some cases,
some names, and locations have been changed.*

First published by AuthorHouse   3/23/2006

ISBN: 1-4259-2285-6 (e)
ISBN: 1-4259-2283-X (sc)
ISBN: 1-4259-2284-8 (dj)

Library of Congress Control Number: 2006901987

Printed in the United States of America
Bloomington, Indiana

This book is printed on acid-free paper.

Dedication

I dedicate this book in loving, joy-filled memory of my parents, Ed and Romona Clark. They gave me life, they gave me the stories. With overwhelming pride and joy, I share them with you.

Table of Contents

Acknowledgements

I wish to acknowledge some very special individuals for their support, encouragement, faith in my abilities to undertake this project, and their undying and unconditional love.

My special, wonderful, and unique sister and brother-in-law, Sandie and Bill Wayland, who endured countless phone calls and conversations, and ended every one of them with the words, "You can do this, Brother." Your faith and love sustains me.

My brother, David Clark, who loves me enough to allow me to use him as an example of the out of town caregiver and who is responsible for my "Middle Child Syndrome!"

My eternal creature and life partner, Steven Begert-Clark, who read, re-read, read again, and edited every word I wrote. He blessed me by giving me the opportunity to accomplish this wonderful task. Steven, you give me a blessed life by your remarkable capacity to love, your wisdom that goes far beyond your years, and your understanding of my need to write this book.

Our children – Thom and Cathy Clark and Jason and Cyndi Clark who believed that as personal and private as our story might be, it might just offer comfort and insight to others who find themselves on the caregiver journey.

Our grandchildren – Andrew, Tommy III, and Katie who remind me daily that life is a never ending adventure of learning and enjoying life. You continue to teach me that one should never take himself too seriously.

Our nieces, nephews, and their children. Melissa, Kevin and Meghan Crump – Shawn, Stacey, Josh and Ryan Wayland – Chris, Mike, Michael and Stephen Palmer - Lori, Joe, Katie and Joey Stephan – who brought such joy into my parents' lives and continue to offer me that same gift.

My extended family – Debi and George Fynes, Karla and Alice Simpson-Casagranda, Judy, Kandy and Klara Haines-Hricik, Emil (Butch) and Amy Perunko, and Diane Clark. Without their humor, love, friendship, encouragement and prayers, the journey about which I write in this book would have been very sad and lonely indeed.

And finally, to Debi Fynes, Alice Simpson-Casagranda, Jackie Ruhlman, and Tommie Ruehr who offered their time, support and comments as readers and editorial advisors during this entire project.

I have been told often that I write like I speak – sometimes too much! So I'll stop here and simply and briefly say once again . . . Thank you.

A Note From The Author

WOW! You've purchased my book! I'm so humbled and truly excited. Thank you for allowing me the opportunity to share with you a little about my family and our journey in caring for our parents. As I sat writing in my home office under self imposed house arrest, I had a wonderful and often challenging time in revisiting old memories and events that molded and shaped this book. I searched my heart and soul to find reasons, or educated guesses at least, for why things happened the way they did. I've taken very few literary liberties in recounting those events (it really did go the way you'll read it) in hopes of sharing a tear, a smile, a memory, a chuckle and maybe even a few belly laughs.

Rosie John Doesn't Live Here Any More...One Family's Journey in Eldercare is my travel log of the up and down, twisting and turning roller coaster ride that was caregiving for me. I would have done well to remind myself before beginning that I am petrified of roller coasters! Nonetheless, I went on the ride and I have no regrets. What a rewarding and deeply emotional experience. My sincere hope is that after taking my book to the register, carrying it to your home and reading it, you'll too feel no regret for having done so.

The stories contained here recount some of my childhood memories and how so much of that influenced my adult life as a caregiver. Some of them you many find to be rather un-splendid, some are sad, others are humorous. None of them individually is meant to give all of the answers you may be seeking – after all, who has all the answers? My hope is that after our visit you'll take away something that will affirm your personal journey.

So get a cup of tea or coffee, or crack open a "tasty adult beverage" and join me as I take you home for a visit with my family.

Tom Begert-Clark
February, 2006

Prelude

When you hear the word "caregiver" what images come to your mind? A husband who has suffered a stroke; a wife with Parkinson's disease; a mother-in-law with cancer; a grandfather with Alzheimer's disease; a son with traumatic brain injury from a car accident; a child with muscular dystrophy; a friend with AIDS?

Currently in the United States nearly one out of every four households, 22.4 million, is involved in caregiving to persons aged 50 and over. By the year 2007, that number could reach 39 million.

The impact of caring for a loved one takes on an entirely new life when we examine the "working caregiver." 25% of all workers are currently providing some type of elder care. Among working people who are caring for a loved one or friend aged 65 and older, two-thirds report having to rearrange their work schedule, decrease their hours or take unpaid leave in order to meet their caregiving responsibilities. Working caregivers deal with the day to day stress of taking care of a loved one and deal with their employer who is not happy that, once again, the workday schedule has been disrupted.

Caregiving is an emotional journey of mountaintops and valleys. Our mountaintops are found in the knowledge that in caring for our loved ones we are given the awesome opportunity to demonstrate our love and commitment. Our valleys are found in exhaustion, inadequate or complete lack of knowledge in regard to available resources, and round-the-clock care – all of which can lead to burnout, stress and depression.

As we were growing up, our parents taught us that we could do anything. Well, let me tell you that if my own siblings and I discovered nothing else in our caregiving journey it was that we really could give excellent care – but we couldn't do it alone! It literally took a team of doctors, social workers, adult day professionals, extended family and friends (a village, perhaps?) and the list goes on and on.

As is too often the case, the caregiver in the home dies before the loved one for whom they are providing care. Such was the case with my own parents. Mom and Dad had been married for over fifty-seven years. They cared for one another for most of that time, but Mom truly became Dad's "live-in" nurse and primary caregiver for much of the last ten years of her life. She died August 11, 2002 . . . before Dad. Dad died fifteen months later – medical diagnosis, "natural causes" – Spiritual cause of death, a broken heart. Both Mom and Dad prepared us – my older sister Sandie, younger brother David, and me – for their departure from this world. They told us plainly, each before the journey, "I love you all . . . you have been so good to me . . . but I want to go home. I am proud of you."

Our hearts were broken and we came to the devastating realization that, although we had had to take control of the soap opera that is caregiving over the last few years, it was our parents who were in control of the ending. Only they could write the final chapter. Only they knew when it was time. Having accepted that fact, the only thing left to do was to send them off with well-wishes for the journey. If they didn't know how much we loved them, how proud of them we were, and how much we would miss them, it wasn't for lack of trying to express it. Those hospital and nursing home conversations were some of the most earnest and heartfelt that I have ever had and I'm glad I was given the opportunity to have them. To this day we continue to miss our parents – that will never end – but we are so grateful for the time that we were able to give back to them and the knowledge we have gained from being caregivers.

If you are a caregiver, you do not have to "go it alone." The mere fact that you landed in the section of your local book store that led you to this book is healthy proof that you are seeking companions to accompany and assist you on your journey. There are people, resources and information available. It is as simple as doing a word search on Google or Yahoo for "Caregiving," "Elder Services," "Caring for a parent/spouse" and the like. Look in your phone book and call your local adult daycare center or senior center. Contact your local Area Agency on Aging (usually found under Social Services).

Remember caregivers, if you truly believe that you want the best for your loved one or friend, you must also believe that your needs are just as important as theirs. If you try to "go it alone" and your health suffers, who will be there to take your place? Denial of your own needs could kill you – that's a fact, blunt but true. Caregivers must balance their needs in order to fulfill the needs of the *caregiven* (for the remainder of the book, that's how I'll refer to your loved ones for whom you are caring – Caregiver, that's *you*. Caregiven, that's *them*.)

The balance of love and caregiving is a wonderful, heartwarming and often a humorous journey. My family does not regret a single moment of the time we spent or the sacrifices we made. We developed an awesome respect for those who were companions on our journey and those who supported our desire to be the best caregivers possible. Every day we looked for something we could smile or laugh at. In our home, laughter truly is the best medicine for anything that might ail us.

Join me now as I share my journey as a caregiver for my parents. What follows is basically a travel log of the up and down, twisting and turning roller coaster ride that is caregiving. Mine is similar to many other stories, I'm sure. But the fact is, it's *mine* and I want to share it with you in hopes that some little thing I say might inspire you to some greater thing that you'll do in your own journey. With sincere apologies to my sister, Sandie and my brother, David – for all those times you said "Don't tell anyone!" Consider it done. I didn't tell anyone – I told *everyone!* Don't worry, no one is going to jail – we did nothing illegal – but we surely would have failed miserably in our screen test to be the "Cleavers!" Face it, we were and are a pretty normal family – what a relief. Family dynamics and situations that arise in caregiving are as varied as the flowers in an English garden. Each individual flower holds no great splendor – but collectively they become something that is magnificent and beautiful. The stories contained here are not much different. None of them individually is meant to give all of the answers. But considered as a whole, I hope that the big story paints a big picture and that you'll take away some good suggestions and tips for your own journey. If nothing else, I hope that my story helps you to put everything into some new and proper perspective. Like raising children, it's difficult to say which approach is right or wrong, better or worse. You simply fly through with a compass and a map and pray that the weather cooperates! So use this book as your map, or your compass, or your umbrella. God knows that when it comes to caregiving, Mother Nature – not unlike the caregiven – is not always on her best behavior.

Never Having to Bring a Casserole

When I was in my early forties I was employed as a HUD Service Co-ordinator for a large independent senior housing complex in Cleveland, Ohio. One day one of my favorite residents came to see me. I know, we aren't supposed to have favorites! But in the social services field, that's a tall, and mostly unachievable, order. Miss Sylvia had something special, wonderful and unique about her that caused people to rise from their seats out of complete and total respect when she entered a room. Her genuine love and concern for her fellow residents could be felt as she spoke to folks in the halls and on the elevators. She would always ask how things were going and would end every conversation with, "Just let me know if I can help out." The community of seniors living in that building simply loved her and I truly don't think that it had anything to do with the fact that she was one of the few residents who could still drive a car! She prided herself in driving other residents around town to shop, keep physician appointments or to enjoy a local restaurant. She was a sharer of her blessings and the torchbearer of the "Golden Rule." If people would do only one half of what Miss Sylvia did unto them, the world would be a wonderful place.

During this particular visit to my office, having first discussed some of her latest aches and pains (normal conversation within the senior housing communities), she said, "Tom, let me tell you something."

Thinking that she wanted to share a concern about another resident, which she often did, or that she would ask me to "quietly look into a situation" that was occurring at the building, I said, "You know you can, Miss Sylvia."

She continued, "Tom, someone once told me never to get old. And I didn't listen. Too hard-headed I guess. But I'm telling you in hopes that you will listen."

I shared the story with my family and friends but soon forgot the conversation. That was until events in my life began to bring me back to Miss Sylvia's words of wisdom.

On August 11, 2002 my mother passed away. My mom and dad had been married for over fifty-seven years and, as is so often the case when one's eternal creature (that's what I call my spouse) passes away, my dad died of a broken heart on November 8, 2003. It was then that Miss Sylvia's simple but profound words came to my mind . . . "Don't ever grow old." Recalling those words and saying goodbye to my parents flung me immediately into this place called "reality." No longer would I be able to say to my sons, "Go ask your grandparents." No longer was I the "son," my sons the "grandsons," and their children the "great-grandchildren." It all changed. I was being forced into getting older. Help me, Miss Sylvia, help me! I want to listen to your advice, but circumstances aren't letting me. What a world, what a world! I had become, through the simple course of nature, the patriarch of my family. I had, in so many areas of my life, taken on the persona of Peter Pan. I blame Miss Sylvia for my refusal to grow up. And the kids loved that – "You're fun, Dad. We're going to grow up together . . . forever!" they would shout. Sadly, Peter Pan was about to embark on puberty.

My father was always there – serving alone as the pillar of guidance and wisdom in our family. What the heck, he had eighty years of experience – why shouldn't he have the job? But here I was, ascended to the throne at only fifty-one! I was beside myself, thinking, "Why did he have to die? Well, we aren't the royal family; there will be no succession to the throne. This commoner will remain so – "King"dom does not become me!" But as the days and weeks went by, I began my royal pilgrimage to assume the figurative and mystical throne where rests the weary behind of the "Patriarch of the Family."

Oh, the family was so slick. It all began quite subtly. It started with phone calls seeking my advice. The adult children of the family asking me to recount stories of when they were toddlers. Invitations to attend every celebration of life – birthdays, baptisms, holidays and holy days – so that I could tell the stories. But there was a catch – a perk, even. I didn't have to bring a casserole! And that's when I knew for sure. Only one person gets away with not bringing a casserole – only one person gets to hear those magic words, "Don't bring a thing, just yourself." That person used to be "Grandpa." Now it was me. I should have seen it coming. Every call, every request, every invitation to a family function and no casserole? They loved my cooking. The buzz would begin days before the gathering about what "Dad" or "Uncle Tom" would be bringing. They know that I'm a TLC cooking show junkie and wondered who would be coming with me to the party – Paula Dean or Bobby Flay. But not any more . . . they only wanted me. Every action premeditated and calculated by my children, nieces, nephews and siblings, moving me ever closer to the throne. Never before had I seen such manipulation and planning from those I loved, cherished and trusted. I actually think they called a conclave and discussed "winning me over," plotting various and sundry guilt trips to send me on if I refused "the honor." Before I could catch my breath or comprehend what was happening, I had assumed my father's role. As I look back, all that was missing was the white smoke rising from my sister's chimney announcing to the family that I had been named my dad's successor. At least the Cardinals have the decency to speak with the candidate first to ensure he is interested in being the Pope!

But there I was . . . and here I am. The part about not bringing a casserole – I like that. It truly is a place of honor. Of course, I still bring one most times. On whom else would I test my latest concoction? But all else that comes with it? Still tough – still a great responsibility and one that I pray I'll do even one-tenth as well as Dad had. If I do even that well, I can just hear him now . . .

"Ah, honey . . . you done a great job."

Thanks, Dad – I needed that.

White Cotton Socks,
Johnson's And Linoleum

Each morning throughout our elementary years Mom would come into our bedroom to wake her children for school. She would softly awaken us with words like "It's time to get up for school" or the more Presbyterian greeting, "This is the day the Lord has made – aren't we glad" or the more sing-song rendition, "Good morning to you, good morning to you! We're all in our places with bright shiny faces. Good morning to you!"

No matter the greeting, the routine was the same – the compulsory lifting of our legs and the placement of white cotton socks upon our feet. She would say that she didn't want our feet to get cold when they touched the floor.

Little did I know at that young age that the day would come when my sister, brother and I would wake our parents with soft words and goofy songs as they began their day. Nor could we have guessed that we would be helping them put their white cotton socks on – the "support" kind, that is. Would they smile as we did? Only time would tell. It will always amaze me how everything we learned as children comes full circle in our adult lives.

My mother's life was consumed by her unbelievable desire and drive to be the best mom and wife to ever walk the earth. She always came off self assured and in control of the lives of those she held so dear to her heart.

Okay, I'm being kind . . . she could be downright bossy and quite opinionated! But within that outward shell – the one that looked in control and undaunted by life's little curveballs (the usual suspects like children, husband, job, home, bills) – there lurked in the shadows Mom's incredibly low self esteem caused, for the most part, by her uncontrollable weight.

Mom was heavy – to be politically correct (it's 2006, you know) she was "big boned," "full figured." Political correctness be damned, Mom was fat! Standing four feet ten inches, she once tipped the scale at over 230 pounds. Mom had the unwanted distinction of being the largest mom in my third grade class. I mean no disrespect – it was what it was and the battle to control it was a lifelong one. Mom's physical presence was apparent but it really didn't seem to be a cause of embarrassment to her children, at least not one we ever shared. Mom was always on a diet. This was a behavior that she passed on to two of her children, my sister and me. Mom tried everything from "Weight Watchers" to "TOPS" (to this day I hate French-style green beans and hot dogs, the staples of this diet plan) and even resorted to having her stomach stapled and gastro by-pass surgery. None of these had any long term effects on Mom's weight, but instead contributed to major health issues in her later years.

During one of her particularly determined "I'm going to lose weight even if it kills me" periods, Mom would fix dinner for the family, put it on the table and then proceed to the basement to do laundry. We would ask Dad where Mom was and he'd disgustedly tell us, "You're mom's dieting again." The entire family would remind Mom that we loved her just as she was. When we would ask why she was always dieting she would tell us that she had been heavy her entire life. She would then "slip into" what we thought were meaningless conversations and stories of how her father would degrade her because of her weight and her mother would comfort her with jelly bread.

Mom's girth and her childhood memories of being made to feel insecure and purposeless caused her to overcompensate and to be even more determined to prove to her family and friends that fat people were not lazy. Mind you, with the possible exception of her father early on, no one had ever said this – none of us even thought it. But in her mind it was "what *they* were saying." She was never able to tell me who *"they"* were.

Mom was consumed with caring for her family. But even that wasn't enough to maintain her self esteem. She filled every extra moment of her life as an active leader at Church, the PTA, summer baseball league, her monthly "500 Rummy" card club and caring for every underdog she ever knew. When she wasn't working, organizing and bossing others – yes, she was often referred to as the bossy matriarch of our family – she had an insatiable and compulsive desire to clean. She kept the most immaculate home you could possibly imagine. I kid you not – it was almost scary. We were never permitted to leave our beds unmade in the morning. She would say things like, "You never know what could happen. Why, you could be crossing the street and a car could hit and kill you. I don't want anyone coming into our house and seeing unmade beds."

Killed crossing the street? What a feeling of security and bliss that created in our wee young minds. No wonder I didn't want to go to kindergarten! I didn't know if I would be killed walking those three blocks to elementary school. Or worse, if it were David who had perished, coming home to find our house filled with strangers and hearing them say, "What a shame. And it all happened so quickly. He was just crossing the street, but what a clean house. Why, even the beds are made!"

I guess when children are hit by cars and killed, mourners routinely make pilgrimage to their bedrooms. And imagine if the child were hit but survived! Oh, the embarrassment – people coming to visit the child lying in that unmade bed in that messy bedroom! A lifetime of therapy could never heal the emotional scars. Having learned so early on in life the grave consequences resulting from an unmade bed, I always asked my own two sons to daily make theirs . . . just in case. They didn't do it. But they are making great progress in their therapy and for this I am truly grateful.

The aroma of Clorox Bleach permeated not only every room in our home, but fumes easily escaped to the houses on either side of us. At any time the scent of bleach could be detected by merely walking up our driveway. I'm quite certain that Mom single handedly kept the Clorox Company in business. To this day my siblings and I use Clorox religiously. Mom was so proud that we had carried forth the tradition.

It was while at a friend's house when I was in high school that I saw my first dust bunny. It terrified me! When I told Mom what I had seen, she just shook her head and said, "See how fortunate you are to have such a clean home. Those poor children! Next time you go to visit I'll send over a gift of Clorox. Are your friend's parents "large" people?"

Our home was a very basic Cape Cod. Mom and Dad's bedroom was on the first floor along with our only bathroom (which often created havoc in the mornings) and two dormer-style bedrooms upstairs. Sandie had her own room, and David and I shared the other room. There were two structural distinctions that Mom was extremely proud of and shared with any first time visitors. One, we had real plastered walls and two, the first floor living areas had beautifully hand-polished light oak floors.

Area rugs were not permitted in our house. No way! Mom said that folks who used area rugs were hiding something underneath. Most likely they hadn't heard of Johnson's Paste Wax or were "too heavy" to properly care for their floors. It was those beautifully hand-polished light oak floors that seemed to bring Mom the most excitement and pride. As a child I thought that was weird. But when my partner and I purchased our first home, built in 1927, what do you suppose is the first thing we did? You guessed it – we took up some of the carpet which revealed natural oak floors. And what do I always say to first time visitors?

"Aren't these natural floors beautiful? The previous owners had them covered with carpet. What a shame to hide all that beauty."

Say it with me now – "Mirror, mirror on the wall. I've become my mother after all!"

Every fall and spring while my sister, brother and I attended school and Dad was at work, Mom would hand wax and power buff the floors with Johnson's Paste Wax. It had to be Johnson's Paste Wax – no other would do. I did develop, at an early age, a major issue with those floors. When first polished they became a health and safety issue. OSHA could have had a field day issuing citations regarding the dangers Mom created by her semi-annual waxing ritual. When freshly polished, the floors became like an indoor ice skating rink. We never knew the exact day when Mom would be getting the Johnson's out from the cupboard under the sink. It was as if she wanted to keep the timing of the task a top secret from her family.

Mom never reclined on the sofa.

"Sofas were made to be sat on," she would scold. "If you want to lie down, go to bed!"

The only time she took exception to her own rule, was on floor waxing day. Our house was such that if you walked along the sidewalk in front of the house, you could see the entire living room by peering through the front door. It was on those semi-annual polishing days that Mom would leave the front door open to "let the sun dance over the beautifully, freshly polished floors." On one of those fateful days, I came home from school and could, from the sidewalk, see Mom in full view performing her semi-annual recline on the sofa (insert soap opera vibrato organ sound here). As she lay there staring at her own reflection in the freshly waxed floor, it was like she was in a trance. Upon seeing Mom practically lying in repose, I simply began to cry . . . for I knew what lay ahead. We had all been down this road before – twice a year, every year.

On each and every waxing day, before our feet even crossed the back door threshold, Mom could be heard, "Take your shoes off. I waxed the floors today. And Tom, you be especially careful. The neighbors don't have to have their windows blown out by your screaming when you slip and fall!"

When I fell, I had a reputation for letting loose a continuous high-pitched scream that brought people from blocks away to see who was being murdered. It was uncontrollable and totally embarrassing. David would always get the biggest kick out of Mom telling me to be careful. I looked at Mom's warning as an expression of her love for me – Sandie and David saw it more as an act of protection from their own hearing loss. Sandie was always very cool about Mom's preemptive words, never making comment toward or about me. But David was another story. He was, unlike me, the athlete – the agile and skinny child. He knew how to roller skate and ice skate. This knowledge would benefit him greatly on freshly waxed floors. As for me, I had difficulty walking let alone trying to perform the task on wheels or razor blades. Keeping upright was made more difficult by the fact that I had been "blessed" by the inheritance of my mother's weight gene. David was always excited when Mom waxed the floors. He was actually quite amazing as I recall. We had a formal dining room that led directly into the living room. David would take his shoes off and start running from the end of the dining room, extend his left foot and slide completely across the living room. His lightning speed could be attributed to two things – his strong push off and his trusty foot-wear – those white cotton socks. David would come to a screeching halt only after smashing into the furthest wall in the living room. He would hit that wall with such force that the pictures that hung from it would shake. All the while Mom would be yelling, "David, stop that! You're going to get hurt!"

But that never deterred him – not one bit. In fact, he would then reverse himself and slide through the living room with his arms out-stretched, gliding gracefully around our dining table, and stopping only when he smashed into the furthest dining room wall. His performance would continue for several minutes until Mom would become angry.

"David, if you don't stop that I'm going to get up and beat the living tar out of you!"

David, being David, kept it up. When Mom had had enough, she would rise – or should I say attempt to rise – from the sofa in order to reprimand her youngest. You see, she would wear these soft bottom slippers so as not to scratch her beautifully hand-polished light oak floors. Her footwear had absolutely no traction. She never wore street shoes in the house as they would surely leave a mark on the floors! And if that happened, the only way to hide the flaw would be with an area rug. There would be no area rug. As she made several attempts to get up, her feet would begin moving in different directions and back down onto the sofa she would go. Although not as orchestrated as David, several times Mom's arms too would be outstretched as if reaching for an imaginary rope or bar for support. It was borderline artistic. The Russian judge gives it a 9.5! The crowd goes into a frenzy over Mrs. Clark's interpretive performance! All the while David would become braver. As Mom tried to get up, David would slide all the more trying to see how close he could get to Mom without her being able to grab him. As Sandie and I stood on the edge of the linoleum separating the kitchen from the freshly polished floors, Sandie's concern for Mom's safety would overcome her and she would begin yelling at David.

"You better quit! You're going to make Mom fall and then you'll get it!" How ridiculous for Sandie to utter such threatening words to our baby brother. Mom couldn't even get to her feet let alone stand a chance of catching David. If she fell, David could continue to slide all around her like a professional figure skater. Once she kissed Mr. Johnson on the floor, everyone knew she would be down for the count and David would never be caught. Now, that line of thinking always got me in trouble. "Why?" you might ask. Because I too would get caught up in the moment and begin to laugh and cheer David on.

"Try to do a figure eight! I'll give you my lunch money if you can get within six inches of her and she doesn't grab you!"

It always amazed me how the utterance of those words would instantly shift the attention away from David and toward me. Mom could never get to her feet to catch Orville Wright's evil brother flying past her, but somehow she always managed to get vertical and begin her trek toward me! Now I knew from past performances that there wasn't a snowball's chance that Mom would get within an arm's length of me, but that parental look and the sheer determination smeared across her face made my heart jump out of my chubby little chest. I always had in the back of my mind that today could be the day – there's a first time for everything – today she could connect! That fear of her possibly reaching me brought out the basic "fight or flight" instinct in me. Needless to say, I chose "flight!" In my panic, I would seek my escape by the only path I thought reasonable. It was a direct path from the security of the linoleum across the living room floor and out the front door. I know what you're thinking. Why didn't I just turn around and exit over the safety of the kitchen linoleum and out the back door? My response is simple. Fear takes over one's mind in these situations and one becomes totally stupid, thinking only of self preservation which has absolutely no connection to intelligent response.

Mom would miraculously get to her feet and, with an ever so slight push of her right foot, arms semi-gracefully extended to her sides, would begin to shuffle across the floor in my direction. It was like time was standing still – everything seemed to be in slow motion. I was about to die. Had I made my bed? Picture it if you have the stomach; nine years old, 130 pounds, four feet tall! I was, for all intents and purposes, the third largest thing in the living room, if you count the 1940's style nylon tweed sofa that sat along the inside wall, and my mother. Two large bodies converging even at slow speed would spell my skinny brother's demise if he were somehow caught up in the collision. He would surely perish in the aftermath and I knew for a fact that *his* bed wasn't made! A limb would be cut from the family tree and my father's lineage would come to an abrupt end.

Our eyes were huge, our arms flailing about as we approached one another. And I . . . well, I was screaming, of course. I knew this could be the end. As the laws of physics dictate, Mom and I collided! Much and always to my surprise, Mom actually had never desired to physically harm me. She simply wanted to use me as a support for her own retreat to the safety of the linoleum. Once we intersected and connected, Mom would start laughing,

"Tom, pull me to the kitchen!"

As if I had not been traumatized enough, the entire epic was revisited when Dad returned from work. The back door opened, Mom sent out the decree to take off his shoes, and Dad would head toward the living area in his white cotton socks to inspect his beloved wife's efforts. With his first step onto the oak floor we heard two sounds - Dad hitting the floor and his most famous response to any occasion that required swearing, "Rosie John!" Following a speedy and remarkable recovery, Dad, the consummate southern gentleman raised in West Virginia, would gain his wits and composure. Sitting spread eagle on the floor, he would look over to Mom standing in the safety of her kitchen and simply say, "You did another outstanding job on the floor, honey!"

Johnson's Paste Wax in the 1950s? Seventy-nine cents. The memories of floor waxing day at the Clark's? Priceless . . .

It Could Always Be Worse

My father worked for a large manufacturer. He was a tireless and loyal employee of General Fireproofing. General Fireproofing was one of the largest manufacturers of office equipment in the United States. Dad worked as a paint sprayer on an assembly line which produced metal filing cabinets.

In the early1960s the company, as did so many other companies, came upon very difficult economic times. Layoffs were common and lasted for months at a time. Over a three year period Dad worked maybe four to six months.

Although he and Mom never discussed the struggle it was to pay the bills and raise three young children on unemployment, I look back and can see the strain that was especially present when we would ask to buy something out of the ordinary. Like most parents, they hated to tell their children no. But their positive outlook rooted in their strong faith and belief that things could always be worse, kept them joyful as well as hopeful.

I realize that it might be difficult for some people to ask for help. Mother was no exception. She believed that she was more than capable of doing everything herself and never would she so much as hint that she might need help. It was during this economic uncertainty that Mom took full time employment as a PBX Operator for a large medical answering service. What a transition that was! Mom had always been a "stay at home" Mom. But again, the positive manner in which this change in our lives was handled by our parents made the adjustment smooth and uneventful. She would often tell us that change was good and that it made us better people.

Dad was always looking for odd jobs in his attempts to supplement his unemployment, all the while believing that work would pick up at General Fireproofing. He believed that his loyalty to the company would guarantee his future employment with them. This "slow down" was just temporary, he would remind the skeptics. He would contend, "General Fireproofing has been good to me for many years, so now I have to stand by them."

He refused to succumb to the constant negative news about the company's bleak economic outlook. He cleaned a local tavern, dug ditches for the city street department, and became the custodian of our church. His attitude was that whatever it took to make things better at home he was willing to do.

I will never forget Dad's employment with the City Street Department. He would come home exhausted and dirty, only to make sure his grass was always cut and the windows washed.

"I have to take care of what God has given us," he would tell us.

During these difficult and economic hard times I never heard my parents argue over money, nor the fear they must have felt of losing everything they had worked for. Their spirits were strong and their faith in God even stronger. No matter what the circumstances, they would always remind us and one another . . . it could always be worse. I remain grateful to this day that we never found out what that really meant. I have adopted that philosophy in my own life and have done my best to pass it on to my own children. Thanks, Mom and Dad – sometimes I wonder if it could possibly get any better!

The Church Lady Cometh

One mid-summer day, prior to Mom taking her PBX job, the Church Lady appeared at our home. We kids called her the Church Lady because we never knew her name. She just attended our church and was always very nice to us. Sandie, David and I were playing in the backyard when she arrived.

We stopped playing as we saw the car pull into the drive. The Church Lady smiled, waved out her window and shouted, "Hi kids! Can you give me a hand?"

We eagerly ran to her car to see what she wanted us to do. Mom heard the commotion and came out of the house to see what all the carrying on was about. The Church Lady greeted Mom with a big hug and quietly spoke to her as we stood eagerly by the car awaiting her instructions. One thing I remember is that Mom began to cry – I couldn't imagine why. She only cried at sad movies or when someone died. What did the Church Lady say to her to bring on the tears? More hugs were exchanged and the Church Lady approached the car.

"Kids, give me a hand with these groceries, will you?"

Mom retreated to her kitchen to prepare for what was about to take place. The Church Lady opened the tailgate of her green 1959 Chevy wagon. We glanced upon what looked like a hundred brown grocery bags filled to their tops. It was like Christmas. What special things did those brown bags hold? Without hesitation we began unloading this cache of goodies. We struggled to carry the overstuffed bags into the kitchen to Mom. We placed the bags on the kitchen table. Mom began to put the food items away as we delivered them. But we were too fast. There were three of us and only one of her. It seemed like we had made fifty trips from the car to the house before we completed our assignment. The kitchen table was now overflowing and bags were being laid on the kitchen floor. We had not seen so many groceries outside of our local Kroger's ever! As we brought in the last bags, the Church Lady said, "Tom, go to the front seat. I have something very special just for you. Be careful bringing it in."

I flew out the door and ran to the car. What could it be? Maybe a toy or perhaps new clothes? The window was down so out of impatience I stood on my tip toes and peered through the open car window. There sitting on the passenger seat was the biggest cheesecake I had ever, or have since, laid eyes on. My favorite dessert of all time! And it was not just an ordinary cheesecake, but one slathered with cherries! Yum! I swung open the car door and ever so gingerly slid my hand under the box supporting that unbelievably delectable treasure. Why, it weighed at least five pounds, maybe ten! As I maneuvered around the car and gently carried the most magnificent cheesecake ever created toward the back door, I could think of nothing else but getting a fork and digging in. It took both arms to support that monster cheesecake. When I got to the back door I yelled, "Help, someone!"

As the porch screen door opened, David and Sandie peered into the box. When their eyes met that cheesecake they gasped. As I entered the kitchen and looked for a place to rest my treasure, I could see that Mom had once again begun to cry.

"Oh my goodness, Tom, your favorite! Set it on top of the stove," she sobbed.

"Mom, don't cry," I said. "You taught us to share. You can have the first piece."

The Church Lady laughed and gave us all a hug.

"Kids, go outside now," Mom ordered.

We ran from the kitchen to take up playing where we had left off. Actually, my thoughts were pretty much with that cheesecake! Would I have to wait until after dinner to begin to devour it? A few moments later the Church Lady waved goodbye as she pulled out of our driveway. Little did I know that if it weren't for our guardian angel disguised as the Church Lady, dinner that night would have consisted of a thin slice of tomato from Dad's small garden nestled between two slices of Wonder bread, with a dab of Miracle Whip. It wasn't until many years later that I realized what a humbling event this was in Mom's life. Mother was the one who always took care of others. She took casseroles and instant Jell-O chocolate pudding pies to shut-ins and those who had some need. As children we were taught by our parents that we were blessed and had an obligation to share what we had with others. God would return our shared blessings ten-fold. And darned if He didn't do it every time.

The circumstances that had been created by no fault of my parents had brought to life the Scripture "You will reap what you have sown." Mom was receiving a portion of her harvest. As children we never imagined that our parents would not be able to take care of their family let alone not be capable of caring for themselves. Children don't concern themselves with such things. But who knew that one day we would take on the role of the Church Lady, sharing in the abundance of our own lives with our parents?

Grounded at Seventy-Six

For months Sandie and I had growing concerns over Dad's ability to continue to drive. Dad was forgetting simple directions and routes that he had driven for years. His ability to drive in traffic or to park the car appropriately at the mall was totally compromised as his judgment and perception dulled.

Mom and Dad lived three miles from the church where they were charter members. They weekly attended choir rehearsals, Bible studies, the men and women's groups and missed very few Sunday services. The church had been not only their spiritual community but the center of their social world as well.

They got their groceries at the same store for thirty years. They could tell you what items were in what aisle. The store was only two miles from their home and they ventured often to make sure the family food pantry was full.

At the onset of Dad's dementia Mom would, as often as possible, accompany him on his normal daily trips to get gas, pick up a loaf of bread or stop by the church. "I'll go along for the ride," she'd say to Dad, always reassuring us that everything was okay because she was with him. But there were those occasions when Dad would simply take the car without informing Mom. Dad loved his car. A 1984 white Oldsmobile with a mere 40,000 miles traveled. He cared for that car as if it were a living being. He washed the car so often that we swore he was going to wash the paint right off its out-of-date chassis. Dad didn't care how cold it was. He would take out his bucket of warm soapy water and sponge in the early morning. If the sun was shining he was going to give his pride and joy a bath. As he would begin to wash the car, the water would literally freeze to the metal. One would think this would have deterred him. Not Dad.

It just made him all the more determined to clean his car, but quickly. When Mom or one of us would sarcastically comment that Dad was just a bit over fixated with the cleanliness of his ride, he always had his pat response, "God wants us to take care of the things He has given us."

"But Dad," I would say – "I don't think God would mind if you skipped the days when the temperature falls below thirty degrees!"

"Feel free to take that to the Lord in prayer!" he would reply. "It certainly would make my job a little easier."

Soon enough, the day that we dreaded had arrived. It was time for Dad to surrender his car keys. Our first chore was to convince Mom of our decision. We firmly and boldly sat Mom down to tell her of our concerns and our action plan. She was aghast.

"I can't do that! It will kill him! You know how much he likes to drive."

Over Mom's objections, Sandie and I knew the keys had to go. If Mom couldn't do it, we would have to.

Dad was scheduled to be hospitalized for a short stay so his medical team could conduct their annual health evaluations. "Perfect," we thought. "We'll make the doctor tell him!" Dad's generation believes everything a physician says. They wouldn't think twice about doubting a doctor's order because they are figures of authority. Yes, even the best of caregivers can become chicken and look for the easy way out. Having difficulty making decisions, taking action? Play the doctor card or get some other authority figure (priest, pastor, rabbi, attorney) to do it for you . . . it's great! The decision is delivered by a neutral party and it's not your fault. It's flawless!

We phoned the doctor's office and explained our dilemma and the doctor agreed to be an accomplice to our plan. Much to everyone's surprise and relief, Dad took it pretty well. He handed his keys over to me as the doctor looked on.

"The doctor knows best," he said. "You know what this means, though, don't you? Your mother will have to drive everywhere now."

There was a brief pause.

"Have you ever ridden with your mother? We're going to be killed."

About two months after confiscating Dad's keys, I received a phone call from Mom.

"Hi Mom. What's up?"

"I haven't slept all night! That's what's up!"

"What's wrong?"

"You're going to be very angry with me. Your father took the keys off the dresser and went for an hour-and-a-half joy ride yesterday."

"What?"

"Oh, don't worry he's fine. He didn't get lost and he's home safe." I sensed sarcasm in her tone. "I'm the one!"

"What do you mean?"

"Well, you know that pound of chocolates you gave me last month?"

"Yes."

"You remember that I agreed to eating only one piece a day?"

"Yes."

"Well, with all the stress yesterday I totally lost it and ate the entire pound! The entire pound, Tom! The sugar and caffeine kept me up all night. Oh Lord, you know what that stuff does to my digestive system. I was up and down all night. Oh sweet Jesus, I thought I was going to die!"

I knew how upset Mom was and it was not the time for a lecture. Questions like, "Why were the keys on the dresser? Why didn't you hide them?" were of no value. I turned to the way I deal with most serious situations in my life. A little humor was in order.

"Well Mom, thank God you're just a chocoholic and not an alcoholic. You could be calling me from the drunk tank!" My mother, the consummate teetotaler responded, "Well, if there's a blessing in this entire event, that's it! Thank you, Jesus!"

That evening we went to Mom and Dad's to hide the keys and have yet another little talk with Dad. Once again we had to "hide" the keys. This time was a little tougher than our first effort. We couldn't hide the keys just anywhere – Mom would forget where we had hidden them and this would only add to her already heightened stress level. I again reminded Dad what the doctor had told him. Wanting to have a dramatic and hopefully memorable ending to our talk with Dad I said, "You know how much we love you. We wouldn't know what to do if anything were to happen to you." In my final effort to make my point loud and clear, I concluded, "You've even said the drivers today are crazy and should be taken off the roads. We agree Dad, but they aren't getting off the roads so that means you better get off the roads." I looked for some type of positive feedback, a sign that he understood and agreed. With Dad's lips tight and sort of twisted, his blue eyes slightly squeezed closed and his hands folded in front of him, Dad's only response was "Your mother is such a tattle tale!" Dad never drove a car after that day.

If payback is sweet, then Dad spent the next few years steeped in honey. In retribution for her "tattle tale" ways on that day, Dad thoroughly enjoyed telling horrifying stories of Mom's driving escapades – near misses here, wrong turns there, a skid mark hither and a close call yon – he would hold court and share all of the details. The grandchildren would roar. Mom would deny every word. And Sandie and I would just eat *Tums* – lots and lots of *Tums*.

Just Take Him To The Undertaker!

Having had his wheels taken away, Dad developed a passion for walking. We encouraged his new hobby – It is an extremely healthy activity both physically and emotionally. Dad would always return from his walks with vivid descriptions of what he saw or found on his morning journeys. Each walk became a sort of adventure for Dad.

In one of the few remaining undeveloped fields at the end of their street, there was a black raspberry patch. It took Dad a few trips through that open space before he discovered this hidden treasure. During the peak season it was not unusual to see raspberry juice seeping through the pockets of Dad's pants, shirt or jacket, incriminating evidence of a good harvest and his impulse to gather unto the storehouse. Scratches from the thorns rendered small bleeding marks on his arms which he wore as proudly as any soldier returning from battle. The tips of his fingers were stained nearly black from the scrumptious juice of the huge berries. Soon Dad was asking Mom for a bucket so he could retrieve more berries for her to turn into jam, a pie, or a cobbler.

On one particular day, Dad returned home visibly saddened because he had spotted heavy equipment – dozers and backhoes – poised to move the earth that cradled his beloved berry patch. The expansion of their condo complex was about to begin. "Soon there won't be berries or fields anywhere," Dad lamented. "People are so greedy. Why do they need to build more condos? The first ones they built aren't even full."

There were also apple trees lining a portion of his walking route. Improper care and pruning of the trees over the years had caused the ill shaped branches to strain as they clung with all their might to their small, imperfectly shaped apples. But Dad's eyes saw not one mark or any discoloration on these delectables – They were wonderful apples to be picked and enjoyed. This story always reminds me that Dad viewed every human being in the same manner – useful, beautiful, rich, delicious even. Dad looked for the good in every person and was rarely unsuccessful in finding it. But back to the apples. Dad soon began carrying blue plastic grocery bags with him on his walks – Far easier was it to carry the payload home in these than in his pockets. He should have thought of that when berries were in season! Like a jeweler carefully setting precious stones, Dad would gingerly pull the apples from the lowest branches, gently laying them in the bottom of his plastic satchel. "So they don't get bruised," he would say. It was as if he were taking pity on these little orphaned apples. Surely they had been through enough as was apparent by their small, sometimes odd shapes, and out of respect, they were worthy of at least one act of comfort and compassion before heading to Mom's pie pan. Another of Dad's inimitable characteristics is that he was the greatest respecter of persons I have ever known. Even people who, in my imperfect mind, had not earned Dad's respect, were granted it by him because "they're a child of God, honey – just like you and me. Ain't nobody perfect, honey – I should know." And then he would laugh as if to say, "I know you don't get it – someday you will." Still waiting, Dad – still waiting.

Dad was still steady on his feet but was beginning to experience more frequent incidents of unsteadiness – ones that would cause him to walk unevenly or even to trip. Sandie and I were constantly reminding Mom to walk with Dad because of our concern that he might stumble and fall, or possibly get turned around and forget his way home. She would agree to our requests, but to my knowledge, rarely kept that promise. Dad still walked alone most days. Dad was an early morning walker which generally eliminated even the slightest chance that Mom would join him. Although Mom was usually up around 8:00 a.m., she was never fully engaged in the real world until around 9:30 a.m. If Mom had even considered going with him, she was by now at least three hours late for the starting gun! By 9:30 a.m., Dad had long returned from his pre-dawn jaunt and was heading for his morning nap.

Dad's habit of getting up before the sun rose really upset Mom. "Your father was up and dressed at 5:00 a.m. and snuck out of the house for a walk again today!" she would include in her daily report. It was fine if Mom was up in time to see him off. Understandably, it made her a little nervous that he walked alone (gee, I wish we would have thought to suggest that she accompany him so she wouldn't be so nervous!), but at least she knew where he was. But the idea of waking up to find him absent from the condo was terribly unsettling. I always wondered how she knew it was 5:00 a.m. Had Dad left her a note?

"Honey, got up at 5:00 a.m. and snuck out without getting caught. Looking forward to my return and my morning chewing out. Love, Clark."

Or had she rigged some kind of device near the front door that recorded exact times of exit and entry – like the swipe cards used at many modern day offices? Had she hired a spotter who hid inside the bush just off the front deck? Or was it Presslye and Bernice next door? God knows those two never slept! Surely they were ratting Dad out to Mom in secret. I'm convinced that they were on the payroll, reporting Dad's comings and goings directly to Mom just before he would return home. I could just imagine that her informant was careful to give Mom enough time to get out of bed, answer the phone, and then take the report. "Mrs. Clark, Mr. Clark is just now rounding the bend – Estimated time of arrival, ten minutes. Estimated time of departure from house, 5:02 a.m. This ends my report." This ten-minute warning gave Mom plenty of time remaining to remove the toilet tissue from around her head – this was worn, of course, to keep her hair from becoming disfigured during sleep. Mom would be prepared for Dad's return.

Mom would position herself in her recliner and when Dad returned she would tell him that she heard him leave and was up ever since waiting for him to get back. And tossed in for good measure, the proverbial "and I was worried to death!" Dad hated to hear that Mom had been worried, especially if he felt he had been the cause of it. "It's dark. You could have gotten lost. A car might not see you and you could get hurt or, even worse, killed!" Dad would always be apologetic for causing her such distress and would routinely promise not to do it again. The very next morning, the short lived promise would be broken and the cycle would begin again.

Despite Mom's efforts, Dad's morning walking ritual continued. There was but one thing to do – call a family meeting. Dad came to hate those meetings the past few years of his life. He always knew deep down that they were "about" him in some way. And something would be decided that would undoubtedly affect him.

Mom decided that new locks should be installed on the doors. We all agreed. It was our hope that the new locks would at least slow Dad's escape long enough that Mom would hear him and redirect him back to bed or to his recliner for quiet meditation and Scripture study. Dad thought the idea was great because it would add another sense of security when Mom was there alone. But lo and behold, our precious Houdini figured those locks out within thirty minutes of installation and began plotting the next morning's escape to "Clarkland." Again and again he would go out for his unsupervised early morning walks. Our efforts continued as we tried to get Dad to understand the possible consequence of his early morning routine. Dad continued his empty promises to take his morning walks later and Mom her hollow pledge to walk with him. The bubble was about to burst. At one particular family meeting, the frustration Mom was feeling had reached the boiling point. I believe that her overstretched emotions were due in large part to the deadly combination of worry and lack of sleep. Even as children we knew not to wake Mom too early. Cartoons were permitted on Saturday mornings, but the sound had to be off if Mom was still in bed. By age four I had learned to read lips and developed an interest in learning sign language.

Mom also had a hidden agenda in her numerous calls for our intervention. Secretly Mom was hoping that, with any luck, Dad would become so discouraged with our interference that he would no longer want to go on his morning walks. This would also take Mom off the hook from any expectation to walk with him. As Dad repeated his promise to abide by the walking rules, Mom continued interjecting comments that were a dead giveaway for her complete mistrust of his pledge.

"Sure, he says this while you kids are here. But trust me – tomorrow morning it will be another story."

"Dad," we urged. "We know that you enjoy your walks. But we're still concerned about you leaving before the sun is up. Maybe you could go a little later in the morning, say 9:00 a.m."

He replied, "Oh but honey, I want to go before it gets too hot. But, if this will make you all happy then I'll do it."

Feeling pretty good about our efforts and the outcome I believed we had achieved, I had to push the envelope.

"Mom, are you okay with this plan?"

She looked directly at Sandie and me and said in the most hopeless and pathetic tone, "Whatever you say – But I told your father that if the police call me some morning and tell me that he's been hit by a car and he's laying in the ditch and they ask me what they should do, I'm gonna tell them, 'Too late now, just take him to the undertaker!' – what else can I do!?"

She said every word of it without a single breath! It's almost comical now. This story has come up many times since my parents have died and it always gets a laugh from the audience. But at the time Mom was truly scared to death – and dead serious. It occurred to us later that day that what Mom was really expressing here was her true anger at the fact that Dad was not considering the biggest potential consequence of his actions – that if something tragic did happen, he would leave Mom behind . . . and alone. It hurt her that he had not considered that being a widow was not in her plan. It bothered her that every effort that she had made to see to his health and wellness could be trumped by something so completely out of her control – a wayward car, a serious fall or some other tragedy. This caregiver was doing everything she could but the caregiven was not cooperating.

After she made the comment, Dad just looked at Mom. Total shock and amazement covered his entire face. And then came his muffled but effective response, "Rosie John . . ."

It was clear that Dad got it. Dementia or no dementia, he really got it.

All future walks were taken under the safe shelter of sunlight, rather than cover of darkness. And his loving wife – his companion of over fifty years – would, from time to time, walk with him – hand in hand, grocery bags in tow, just in case one berry patch or apple tree had been left in tact.

Cuddling – A "Normal Sexual Activity"

Dad was hospitalized from time to time with multiple health issues, most associated with his diagnosis of Alzheimer's disease. (We came to learn that this was a misdiagnosis – more on that later.) With David living in Atlanta, the responsibility for this adventure in caregiving fell to Sandie and me.

To be perfectly honest – I know you don't want me to lie to you – it was Sandie who was the primary caregiver in most of Dad's hospital stays. Although I tried to be present during his numerous discharge planning meetings, it was rare for me to be there. Sandie took her role very seriously, but she never took herself too seriously. And that, fellow caregivers, is some of the best advice that you'll read in this book or anywhere else for that matter. Take what you do seriously – caregiving can be serious business and has a profound and lasting impact on the caregiven. But surviving it all absolutely demands that you not take yourself too seriously. It's difficult to know the difference sometimes, but those of you who have traveled the road know what I'm talking about. Those of you about to set sail will learn it quickly. Sandie is a registered nurse and was the expert when it came to Mom and Dad's medical care. I always yield to the experts in my life and, as a caregiver, my adherence to that policy was every bit as strong. Yes, Sandie was the expert – but when it was needed the most, she became my sister and my friend – the one I cried and laughed with – the one who brought me back when I would begin to take myself too seriously.

Our mother lived quite vicariously through her children. Mom would always introduce us with our professional titles. "This is my daughter, Sandie, the registered nurse and my son, Reverend Tom, the pastor!" David had long since moved to Atlanta when Mom started this behavior and so never had to endure this ritual of matriarchal pride and gloating. But had he been nearby, I'm quite sure that she would have convinced all to whom she introduced David that the car they were driving was on its last leg and they should buy a brand new one from her son, the TOP salesman at the Ford dealership. Although it could be annoying at times, it came to be of great benefit when Mom was forced to transition from primary caregiver for Dad to secondary caregiver for him. In her mind, she was now leaving Dad's care in the hands of the true experts – her own children, the nurse and the pastor. What could be better? If it weren't for our deep shared love and for the respect Mom shared with us, it might have been a much more difficult transition for Mom.

On one occasion, Dad had been hospitalized for about five days. After a myriad of tests, his physicians would always report to us that Dad was a "very complex case." Translated, this meant that his tending physicians had not a clue what was ailing him and that he would be discharged. For some very unusual reason, Sandie wasn't able to be at the hospital during Dad's discharge that day, but her schedule did allow her to be at Mom and Dad's condo around noon. So, thinking that the whole discharge process couldn't possibly be that difficult, I volunteered to go it alone. I made arrangements to pick Mom up that morning. We arrived at the hospital to bring Dad home around 10:00 a.m. After getting Dad dressed, the discharge nurse came into the room and began to review his "plan of care" and home instructions with us.

"Well, Mr. Clark," she began. "Doctor would like you to call in a few days to schedule a follow up appointment."

Looking at me, Dad asked, "Honey, you'll handle that for me?"

Now, Dad knew that Mom was very capable of handling these tasks, but during times like these he would always defer to Sandie or me. I always believed that this was his way of keeping some control over his care by assigning us to these types of tasks. I smiled and nodded.

"Doctor has also made some med changes. We should begin those today. Are you able to stop on your way home and get them filled?"

Again, Dad looked over at me.

"Honey, can we stop on the way home?"

Again I smiled and said, "No problem, Dad."

And then, without missing a beat, the nurse continued, "The doctor said you may return to normal daily activities." And in a cheery high-pitched voice she exclaimed, "You have no driving restrictions!"

Dad's head jerked up and he began to smile. Mom slumped in her hospital easy chair and I jumped in, "The doctor must have forgotten to write down that he doesn't want Dad to drive for a bit longer – until he gets his strength back and sees how he does on these new meds."

The caregiver now hears the roar of the crowd! I had hit a walk-off home run in the bottom of the ninth! Among the many new skills a caregiver must learn, one of the most useful is the act of thinking very quickly on one's feet and the occasional transference of one's own remedies onto the doctor's clipboard. Okay, I flat out lied. Dad couldn't drive again and I knew it. That the doctor didn't know it wasn't his problem – it was mine and every other driver's on the road, so I had to intervene. In doing so, I had to learn to put aside religious guilt and know that God would not hold me responsible for taking whatever actions necessary to protect my father's safety and our family's sanity. Thank heaven, the discharge nurse was quick to catch on.

"Oh, I missed the doctor's handwritten note at the bottom. Yes, Mr. Clark, no driving until the doctor releases you."

Daddy looked completely defeated but nodded his head in agreement.

At this point I was thinking that the conversation was about to end and I could get Dad and Mom out of there and back home. But, to my dismay, the nurse continued, "But, Mr. Clark, Doctor says that you may continue with all other activities of daily living – walking, eating and normal sexual relations."

NORMAL SEXUAL RELATIONS! I thought my father was going to jump out of his skin with pure delight! I felt like I had been flung into slow motion. My walk-off homer had just been snagged by a seven-foot outfielder reaching over the left field wall! My head turned ever so slowly toward Mom. As my eyes made contact with hers, I could see that she was nearly about to faint. In my professional capacity I had worked with many families regarding this very topic. I was always quite willing to explain to them that normal sexual relations and aging were nothing to fear or attempt to avoid. But these were my parents! I had heard professional sex therapists at several conferences present the latest studies on sexuality and intimacy for elderly when dementia type diseases affected one of the partners and how perfectly normal this was. The seminars flashed back in my mind at the speed of light. Studies had shown that elders in their seventies, eighties, and nineties were still engaged in sexual activities . . . but not my Mom and Dad! And even if they did, I didn't need or want to know about it. I felt light-headed. I began to feel – even hear – a strange, strong, pounding coming from my chest. The room became very warm. I placed both of my feet firmly on the ground hoping to stop the room from spinning. I thought I was going to pass out. Brilliant idea, Tom. You fall on the floor and the attention will be diverted from sex to the guy lying on the floor. The announcement would travel through the halls via the antiquated hospital sound system, "Fifty-year-old who doesn't want to hear about his parents having sex needs assistance in room 628! – Caregiver down, room 628!" As my eyes finally focused on Mom's, both as wide as saucers, she spoke in a tone that I had never heard from her before – It was almost demonic.

"Well, say something, Tom! Tell your father that there will be none of that going on in our house!"

Tell him? I couldn't even take in enough air to make the gasping sound that normally precedes one's death and she wants me to "Tell him, Tom?" I'm practically hyperventilating and she calls for the abstinence lecture? And she just kept saying it – over and over again – in short detached phrases.

"Forget it . . . Tell him, Tom . . . There will be none of that!"

Then, without warning – like being rear-ended in traffic or hearing an explosion – Mom took it completely to the house and right through the roof when she said,

"And besides, Clark (everyone called Dad "Clark"), you know I have a fallen bladder and I'm not up to having it surgically repaired! Tom, tell him!"

"Oh please, Mom! What do you mean you have a fallen bladder? Fallen where? Never mind – I am not going there and you can't make me!"

The blood rushed from my face and I lost the feeling in my legs which meant that fleeing the room was out of the question. My thoughts immediately turned to Sandie, the RN, my fellow caregiver, my strength in difficult times, my sister who was at Mom and Dad's condo getting lunch ready – oblivious to the fact that her little brother was having a stroke! With my eyes glazed over and my mouth hanging open to expose fifty years of dental work, I gazed at the discharge nurse hoping that she would offer words of understanding and sanity, support and assistance. When this finely trained expert finally spoke, all she could muster was, "You're on your own on this one."

Where in "Caregiver For Your Parents 101" was this topic covered? In what chapter would I find the wisdom to handle this occasion appropriately? On what page was the diagram showing me step by step how to redirect? And what exactly is a fallen bladder? At that moment in time I wanted to return to my adult daycare center and its participants. I longed to hear their arguments over how Miss Bea was cheating during the morning bingo game and therefore winning all the prizes. I wanted to hear George talk about WW2 – "The Big One" – and how he just knew that with all the problems going on in the world he would, any day now, be receiving his letter from the Defense Department informing him that he was being recalled to active duty at the young age of eighty-four. I needed to return to my comfort zone. I needed my frail, demented friends at the adult day center to keep me grounded in their reality so that I could escape mine. Being a man of faith, I said a silent prayer looking for divine guidance and an appropriate response.

"Please, God, give me the right words to de-fuse this situation!"

The words didn't come as quickly as I wanted. After what seemed like an hour, I felt my mouth form the words that would take care of this once and for all. I trusted it was the Lord who was giving me those holy and comforting words and finally they poured forth from my lips:

"Dad, what the doctor means is that you and Mom can cuddle . . . you know, to stay warm."

Cuddle? Where in the world did that come from? I had called upon the "author" of the best selling book of all time and he gave me this? It was clear to me at that moment that even God suffers at times with writer's block! I had hoped that Dad's dementia and Mom's hysteria would somehow make the "cuddle" word bring them to their senses and calm the situation. After all, the word must have come from God . . . there was not a chance in the world that I could have come up with "cuddle" acting alone. And then Dad, in a moment of complete lucidity and coherency, said to Mom, "Oh, for heaven sakes, honey – I was only pulling your leg! Rosie John!"

At that very split second the discharge nurse handed me Dad's discharge papers, called for a wheelchair, and said,

"Have a safe trip home Mr. Clark."

She then leaned over to me and whispered, "I'd love to be a mouse in your car on this trip home!"

She laughed that "you made my day" kind of laugh and walked out of the room. I imagined that my folly would get top billing back at the nurse's station or in the cafeteria. So I had managed to make someone's day and Mom and Dad were going home to "cuddle." An honest day's work, to be sure.

The silence on the ride home was deafening. While sitting in that nonverbal-ness, I just kept thinking that my father had never even said the "s-e-x" word, let alone talked about or made light of the act. I realized that I had, from my youngest years, been in total denial that "that" had never taken place following the conception of David. I was convinced that it was on that date nine months prior to June 4, 1953 that my parents had entered into an a-sexual contract never to engage in or speak about the subject again.

I stopped at the local pharmacy to get Dad's prescriptions filled.

"I'll be right out. No fighting!"

Mother was sitting in the front passenger seat and just folded her arms. Her pocketbook hanging from one arm, Mom refused to look anywhere but straight ahead. The scene in the car did little to convince me that my "no fighting" decree would be obeyed. Dad, on the other hand, was in the back seat wearing a Texas sized grin. It was a childish, devilish look that I remembered seeing on Dad's face when I was a child when he knew he had just gotten Mom's goat. It was priceless.

When we arrived at the condo, Sandie was waiting at the front door with a great big smile. Mom entered first walking quickly by my sister without even a "how-do-you-do." The look of disgust on Mom's face, the likes of which I had never seen before, told Sandie that something did not go well. Conversely, Dad was practically running up the walk to greet my sister. It was like he had a new spring in his step, a new lease on life. Oh the humanity! As he entered the condo he said, "And how's my favorite daughter?"

He gave her a huge hug and kiss and proceeded to the bathroom. I entered last. Sandie looked at the terror in my face and asked, "What's wrong? Are you alright?"

"I am totally exhausted and we need to talk! I am never going to do this by myself again. If your schedule doesn't allow for you to be at a discharge, then, I'm sorry, Dad will just have to stay in the hospital until you can be there! And one more thing, Miss Registered Nurse . . . What the _hell_ is a fallen bladder!?"

It was on a visit to see Mom and Dad a few weeks later that I discovered that they were now sleeping in separate bedrooms. Not thinking, I asked why. With a stern look on her face and pointing her finger directly at me, Mom retorted, "We both just sleep better!"

Clearly, "cuddling" had not gone over well.

Caregiver Martyrdom

Some forty-four years later the Church Lady came back to my mind. Mom was in need of some serious help as Dad's daily care was becoming more challenging. But Mom had developed "caregiver martyrdom." This is a condition recently discovered by this book's author, which causes caregivers to refuse all offers of assistance, because to do so would be a sign of weakness and would further render them purposeless and, therefore, unneeded. It develops when the caregiver becomes so steeped in the task that it becomes his/her entire purpose – thoughts of taking a break or leaving some part of the chore to others are summarily dismissed and suddenly the whole event, the entire thing, becomes about the caregiver rather than the caregiven. The martyr wants no help, but complains endlessly that there is no help. Because Mom suffered with this "disease," she refused most every offer we would make to help. "I can do it myself," she would say – And most of the time she did and she did it well.

In the last years of Mom's life, she wore her martyr's crown (or was it a tiara?) proudly. She always put up quite a good fight when it was suggested that she needed help. In her last two years, she never resisted an opportunity to complain and lament how difficult it was for her to care, day in and day out, for Dad. Then, just as proudly and loudly, she would reject any assistance. As she put it, "It was her cross to bear."

Okay – that's settled – no one can care for Dad as well as Mom does, so we'll shift gears. Instead of offering to help, let's try introducing the notion of "caregiver respite" – let's give Mom a break today. After all, her daily mantra "I never go anywhere – I'm stuck in this house all day" had, by now, a recognizable melody to it – one that you sing over and over in your head while trying to fall asleep. But when sleepless family members – children and grandchildren alike – would get the hint and reluctantly offer to take Mom out, she would refuse saying, "Well, I can't leave Dad!"

(Cue urge to scream.)

When the offer was extended to take both of them on the outing instead – "You know, Mom, we can all go, but this would just give you a little break," – she would say, "Forget it – I need to be away from him!"

(Cue urge to jump.)

Often when visitors would stop in the late morning or afternoon, Dad would be in bed but Mom would refuse to wake him because "he was so tired."

(Cue urge to bang head on flat hard surface.)

And most any visit by most anyone included the oxymoronic admonition from Mom, "No one ever comes to visit."

(Cue urge to call financial advisor and check on life insurance policy!)

On one occasion, Sandie actually convinced Mom to allow her to take Dad for the day to give Mom a break – she must have promised her chocolate upon their return! When Sandie and Dad returned and shared the day's events, Mom became irritated. She was plainly jealous that Dad had had a good time and she had stayed at home. It reached the point where we all began to wonder aloud if there was any pleasing Mom. Could we ever do enough, could we ever get it right, would she ever be happy, were we really that bad? A martyr has the uncanny ability to make a person truly consider committing . . . well . . . martyrdom!

Caregiver martyrdom is actually very common. Mom didn't invent it – she worked hard to perfect it but it was really nothing new. And when you truly understand it, it is incredibly easy to recognize and to forgive. The fact is, its biggest cause is simply caregiver exhaustion. Caregivers become so tired they simply don't realize that they are in trouble. They sometimes don't know where to get help because there is, in their minds, no time to even look it up. The simple truth is that, for many caregivers, time is just a blur. Hours run into days, which spill over into weeks speeding full boar into months and even years. Listen to a caregiver share stories of his/her journey. "So last Tuesday . . . or was that Wednesday . . . or was it October, Christmastime – yes there was snow on the ground, I remember that . . . Oh, I dunno, whenever it was – anyway, I'm driving Dad to the doctor and . . ." Time just marches on and on. And for the caregiver, time is precious. Every caregiver slips into and out of "time is running out" mode. Is it any wonder that they want to be present for every possible moment . . . in time?

Mom would complain to me that Sandie hadn't been there on a particular day. Mom would inform Sandie that I hadn't called. Sandie and I had such a great relationship, it was easy for us to recognize Mom's complaints for what they were – martyrdom. Another issue with caregiver martyrs is their underlying theory that no one could possibly take care of their loved one better than they can. And the martyr goes to great lengths to be sure that no one is ever given the opportunity to possibly disprove this theory!

Sometime during 2000, I began to hear something in Mom's voice that I hadn't heard before. It was the sound of total exhaustion and depression. This matriarch who had held our family together during all the difficult times by her endless energies, talents and royal commands seemed to be nearing the end of her rope. But even then, she refused help each and every time it was offered. She had become negative and angry. Her total outlook on life was all but hopeless. Mom felt she had no control over her life or the situations that arose within it. Her life was nothing more than the monotonous day to day, week to week care for Dad.

Mom had dealt for years with Dad's early diagnosis of dementia. She had not only assumed the responsibility of his total care, but continued to care for everyone else in her family and circle of friends. Unless Mom was caring for someone she didn't seem happy. As much as we would encourage Mom to be with healthy and happy people, she was like a magnet attracted to those who were ill, unhappy or in need. Caregiving gave her purpose and the strong sense of being needed. It was an escape from her world into the world of someone else's often sadder adventure. Remember, things could always be worse and Mom seemed to fill her life with people who could prove it. Mom would pray for God to intercede and help these less fortunate people. But never did she pray for herself. Yet when her prayers for others were answered and someone's situation improved, she seemed almost unhappy because her work was finished.

Mom was always very opinionated – who isn't, really? But in her later years, Mom had less and less trouble sharing those opinions with any who would listen. I've come to realize that, as folks age, the tendency to share opinions is also pretty natural. Even Dad, in his later years, was far more vocal regarding family life, politics, religion and the like. But there was a certain negativity in Mom's expressions that revealed her exhaustion and her discontent with what she felt was her "lot in life" – caring for Dad and trying to keep everything, and sometimes everyone, under control. Though it was clearly a cry for help, her behavior most often caused isolation and at least mild rancor among the family. Sandie and I spent much time explaining to our own and David's children that this was just "Grandma being Grandma," and urging them try to understand what she was going through – prodding them to "walk a mile in Grandma's shoes." And they did just that – trying to visit their grandparents as often as possible and involving them in "rite of passage" moments such as weddings, baptisms and other family feasts. It wasn't always easy, but we are so proud of our children for seeing through Grandma's hard exterior and understanding that, agree or disagree, she deserved their respect and that she loved them very much.

After months of swallowing words and having our own pride and self-worth fed to us by St. Ramona The Martyr, Sandie and I finally arrived at that watershed moment that is at once necessary, but at all times undesirable. It was time for the dreaded "role reversal" – when the children say to the parent, "Enough is enough." It was time for us to take control of the situation. True enough, Dad's health was declining. But even more painful to watch was the slow and painful death of Mom's spirit. We could not allow that to happen. Intervention was imminent – and had we known then what we know now, we would have brought an attorney to the meeting! This was going to be one tough case.

The Uninvited Guest

The family had gathered for the annual Christmas party. Food, fun, and new babies who had arrived throughout the year filled Mom and Dad's home. Clark Christmas gatherings had been a tradition since the day I was born – I don't remember celebrating the holidays any other way.

Dad's dementia was becoming more apparent, but he still had control over most activities and functions of daily living. He loved having the family around him. Dad would sit in his favorite swivel recliner with a smile permanently plastered on his face. Every once in a while he would take his cane and try to hook one of the toddlers as they would run by him so he could pick them up and give them some "sugar" – a southern kiss.

I loved being with Dad. His gentle and loving demeanor brought a childlike feeling of security to my inner soul. Like a child, I would cozy up to him at the foot of his chair and rest my arm on his knee – what a feeling of tenderness and closeness that simple act would bring to me.

At this particular Christmas gathering an uninvited guest arrived. Her name? "Reality." And, lo and behold, she brought luggage!

After we had filled our bellies with all manner of holiday goodies, we gathered in the living room for the event of the evening, the annual gift exchange. With the number of participants now over forty, the matriarch – that would be Mom – had devised a plan. Gifts would be handed out from the youngest to the eldest, one at a time, so that everyone could "ooh and aah" as the beautifully wrapped packages were opened to reveal the treasures within. As gift wrapping and tissue paper were flying, and the wee little ones were running and jumping into newly formed colorful mountains, Dad looked down at me. As if he knew that what he was about to say to me might cause him embarrassment, he spoke in a soft whisper, "Honey, now don't get me wrong. I love everyone being here. But whose birthday is it?"

My heart sank. I could feel the smile on my face literally melting. My eyes – the mirror image of Dad's bright baby blues – began to fill with tears.

"Oh my," I thought to myself. "What has just happened?" I thought further, "Tom you've got to recover quickly. You work with these types of situations every day at your adult daycare center. Always expect the unexpected. Flip into your work mode. Come on . . . he's looking for you to respond. Quick! Respond! Dad's looking at you and waiting." Clearing my throat and regaining my lost smile I said, "Well, Dad, it's Jesus' birthday! We're here to celebrate Christmas together."

I gently patted his knee as a sign of reassurance. I pretended that it was no big deal – for his sake. But the great pretender was working hard not to let it show that this was a big deal – a very big deal.

My heart was broken. No one else in the room had heard his softly spoken question. I felt like I was in a room with dozens of my closest family and friends, but I was so alone in the pain that my spirit was feeling. No one could see my heart breaking. No one could hear the crusher bearing down on my spirit. I had hoped that I was invisible. I was glad that Dad trusted me enough to ask, but I was saddened by the fact that he had to. I don't know that I had ever felt so sad at any moment in my life before that. "Reality," the uninvited guest, began that day to make plans to "hang out with the Clarks" for a long time to come – She had cleared her calendar and was all ours. And we didn't even need to book an appointment.

My thoughts began racing again. I had to save him! I had to do something to stop this terrible disease that was consuming my father. If he had forgotten that it was Christmas, how soon would it be before he might forget that I was his son?

After the gifts were opened, Dad always asked for a large trash bag and recruited the little ones to help Great-Grandpa pick up the paper that now blanketed every inch of the floor. As Dad and the kids laughed and went about their task, I pulled my sister and brother out of the living room for an impromptu family meeting. We retreated to one of the bedrooms and I closed the door. After sharing with them the incident and shedding some tears I said, "That's it! Mom needs some help. Dad's disease is progressing and it's not going to get better – only worse."

We decided to take a few days to come up with a plan that would not only help Dad, but that would receive Mom's blessing as well. We returned to the room just in time for Dad to make his annual Christmas speech.

As he arose to speak, I feared that he would slip by thanking everyone for coming to his or Mom's birthday party. If that happened, the entire family would see his confusion and realize that the patriarch was failing. Dad slowly began to rise from his recliner. That was always the cue for Mom to quiet the room.

"Everyone, Grandpa has something to say."

It was almost magical how a hush fell over the room at this moment each year. Even the smallest guests quieted their romp, with little urging from their parents, to give Grandpa their full attention and respect. As Dad stood, supported by the cane he came to call his "friend," he began.

"I want to thank everyone for coming today. Thanks for the presents. Mom and I love when we can all get together for these kinds of occasions. So, from the bottom of our hearts, we thank you and we love you all so very much. God bless you all . . . and . . . and . . . MERRY CHRIST-MAS."

You can exhale, Tom! The *real* Great Pretender had once again given an Oscar-worthy performance. No one in the room except for me, Sandie and David had any idea that only thirty minutes before show time, their beloved husband, grandfather, and great-grandfather had no earthly idea why forty people had simultaneously converged to visit. Although the speech was nearly the same year after year, most of us would get a little misty-eyed because we knew how sincere Dad was in his love for us and how sincere was his thanksgiving for "all that you done *(sic)* for us during this past year."

Yes, over the years Dad had mastered the role of the Great Pretender – pretending to be fully aware of his surroundings and those who occupied the space. But those among us who knew it was an act knew that the dementia was worsening, affecting his life, Mom's and ours. Living with that reality – that rude and uninvited guest – would prove to be the most difficult act of hospitality we would ever endure.

Someone Had To Do It

Being a caregiver may bring about some great physical demands, but the emotional and mental strains can, and usually prove to be, even tougher. Tough decisions that affect caregiver and caregiven must be made and implemented on an almost daily basis. As caregivers we often try for as long as possible to delay life-changing decisions that might rob the caregiven of his/her freedoms and privileges. Taking the car keys is just one among classic examples. And let's face it, part of the delay can be chalked up to self-preservation – none of us wants to be "the bad guy." We caregivers think that our boat doth rock enough just getting through the day. Heaven help us if we do anything so drastic as to cause said boat to sink.

I strongly believe that in the case of a disease like dementia or Alzheimer's, the caregiven appears so physically healthy that often we forget s/he is sick. Dementia patients have a great ability to move in and out of reality. This produces false hope within the mind and heart of the caregiver that the caregiven will one day return to the person s/he used to be. The cold hard fact is that dementia does not go away – it only progresses.

Frustration is often voiced by professionals in the field of geriatric caregiving as families seem to have difficulty in assuming control of a loved one's life, especially one suffering with dementia. We often ask ourselves why the primary caregiver(s) isn't moving quickly to get more help. Why are they wavering over enrolling in adult day services, home health and home delivered meals? Why are they allowing the caregiven to make the final choice as to their care when they are not even capable of telling you what they had for lunch? Some attribute slow decision making to the guilt that is associated with having to make decisions for and about a once very independent and self realized person. If I do decide to put Dad in daycare, am I doing it just to take the "easy way out?" Wouldn't a loyal son just quit his job and stay at home with his father and enjoy every "last" moment together? If I put Mom in daycare, am I really just easing her into acceptance of her imminent voyage to the nursing home? And that's not all. What will others – yes even other family members – say once I've made the tough decisions? When they say that I should be ashamed of myself, will they be right? This emotional battle plays out in your mind, heart and deep into your soul. You've read every book on the matter to prepare for this day, you know what's best for the caregiven, yet you still struggle with the guilt. My own experience and study have revealed to me that, while guilt is appropriate in certain instances, it has no place here – and this is why.

Webster's New World Dictionary defines guilt as "the act or state of having done a wrong or committed an offense – conduct that involves guilt; wrongdoing; crime; sin." Friends, if you think that making these important and life *enhancing* decisions is wrong, criminal or sinful, then you are now about one quarter of the way through reading the wrong "self-help" book and you should retire it unto the shelf of your personal library. Pick it up again only when you come to the realization that you *are* good, that you *do* mean the best for your loved one(s) and it *is* really for the best that you are in charge at this moment. Will you make mistakes? Of course you will – human beings do that from time to time. Is it a mistake to take your role as a caregiver seriously and to do what is truly best for all parties concerned? Absolutely not – It would be sinful . . . I dare say even criminal to do anything less.

Fortunately, my own experience in the adult day industry and my sister's experiences in nursing had taught us to "give up the guilt" long before there was a need for us and my brother to assume the responsibility for the day to day decisions for our parents. We had come to the realization that my parents were moving on in their life journeys and the roads we had all traveled together would be traveled no more. We could all still travel together, to be sure, but there was a fork in the road. And this time, we – not our parents – needed to decide which way to go. Now these were tough decisions – Why me? What if we picked the wrong way? Who brought the map? And if you know my siblings and me, who could read the map even if we had one!? Making the decisions was unsettling, trust me. But being the one to make the decisions was not. Caregivers, begin now to view your role as life-enhancing, even life-saving. View yourself as the blessing that the caregiven so richly deserves. Snuff out the guilt and embrace the truth – Your loved one needs you to take charge at this moment. That truth shall truly set you free – free of guilt, free of apprehension, of worry, fear and anxiety.

When we realized that we needed to become the true caregivers (who else was going to do it?), we quickly found peace and empowerment in our new role. No one said that to be an adult child would be easy. So we simply set our minds and our hearts to the task and worked very hard to ensure that our parents did not feel as though they were losing control over their lives. At every turn we discussed situations and options, but we did not delay in making final decisions if their health or safety was in question. We also learned quickly that this "role reversal" is equally uncomfortable and stressful for the caregiven. We worked very hard to keep their feelings about the matter foremost in our minds – the "walk a mile in their shoes" reminder to self that kept us compassionate and forgiving even in the most challenging situations.

I remember when families would come to my adult day center and we would sit in my office and share for hours about how they, as adult children, were experiencing complete role reversal. Their parents had always taken care of them, but now they found themselves taking care of their parents. I don't remember any regret or resentfulness on the part of these "rookie" caregivers – but I do remember fear, an awful lot of fear, about the decisions they would need to make and just where it would all lead them. The baseline to their stories became almost ordinary.

> *I can't believe it – I have to remind Dad to take his medicine, and I even have to remind him to eat and to take a bath.*

> *I have to go over to my parents' house every day – sometimes more than once a day – just to be sure they are safe.*

> *I go over to Mom's to help her clean and to do laundry but sometimes I have to remind her that it's 2:00 p.m. and she should not be sitting in front of the television still clad in her night clothes!*

Had I but one nickel for every son and daughter who told me that they only wanted what was best for their parents, I would be a very wealthy man. The irony is that in our resistance to making important decisions for our loved ones, we may very well be doing what is worst for them in the long run.

This resistance to decision making would often play out in my office. After coming to full agreement that adult daycare would be the best course for all involved, the bubble – mine and theirs – would burst when one of the siblings would say "Well, let me see what Mom thinks about the idea and then we'll get back to you if she decides she wants to attend."

I can remember wanting to scream, but would gently nudge instead,

"We've spent a great deal of time here today establishing the fact that your mother is not capable of making even the simplest decisions, yet you want her to make this one?"

Then, gently but persuasively, I would continue, "Did you ask your children if they *wanted* to go to school? I think not – You insisted that they did because you were in charge and you knew that it was in their and your best interest. The fact is your responsibility and knowledge as a parent took priority over what your children wanted. You wanted what was best for them and made decisions *for* them for many reasons, but first and foremost because you loved them. I'm not implying that your parents are now children, but the same principle applies – you are in charge because you need to be in charge and shying away from decision making could have a very negative impact on all of you."

This line of reasoning often seemed to make sense and, in most cases, was the "clincher" for sealing the deal. And not one caregiver ever reversed his/her decision after enrolling his/her loved one in adult daycare. Some would discontinue due to lack of financial resources or admission to a long-term care facility, but none ever left just because the caregiver felt s/he had made a poor decision or did not see results.

Caregivers, it is important to treat the caregiven with the utmost respect as you make these decisions – they are not your children and, in sporadic streaks of lucidity, they have an incredible way of reminding you of this fact! Timing is everything. As you take on decision making and become more empowered and comfortable in your new role, you will learn good timing, peaceful but persuasive negotiation, and the art of choosing your battles. Fear not – if you keep the caregiven as your constant focus, even the timing, negotiating and battling will bring you peace because you realize that you are doing your best and doing it for all the right reasons. Let's face it, we want our loved ones to be around us as long as possible. Taking control of the situation now and boldly making decisions will ensure quality and even quantity of life. Use your "adult knowledge" instead of your "childhood response" in making choices that affect the caregiven. Go ahead – do for them what they have done for you. Love them, nurture them, care for them and make the days, months and even years ahead the best that they can be for all of you. I promise that if you do, you might just live long enough yourself for your children to take care of you!

Your Time Is Up, Mrs. Clark

As the days, weeks and months moved on, the situation with Mom's caring for Dad grew dismal. Mom's health, which had not been good for several years, began to deteriorate noticeably. Years of being overweight and family genetics generously contributed to her uncontrollable high blood pressure and elevated cholesterol. Add to these the physical toll of several major surgeries over the years and you have a woman whose physical and emotional batteries had been switched to overload – they were draining fast with little hope of recharging.

Dad had begun to resort to sleeping his days away due to complete lack of stimulation. It was also his method to avoid spending his waking hours in a non-conversational, emotionally dark environment. Unfortunately, this was all quite acceptable to Mom. If Dad was asleep, she too could sleep and fall deeper into her depression. Dad's absence allowed her to spend the time not thinking, not feeling . . . just escaping into a make-believe world of make- believe well being. It didn't matter what time of day or evening we would call, Dad was always asleep. This hibernation was having a major affect on Dad's daily abilities. The more he slept the duller his social skills became. No longer was he able to pick out what he was going to wear. He had no interest, desire or ability to carry on conversations. The last enjoyable activity that Mom and Dad shared was to occasionally go out for dinner. Even this came to a screeching halt due to Dad's inability to recall manners while eating. He wasn't able to select from a menu, cut his food or drink from a full cup of coffee. Friendships ceased to exist due to Mom's persistent negative attitude and Dad's inability to act appropriately in social settings. As cliché as it sounds, Mom had created her own physical and emotional prison. It was not a happy place.

Sandie stopped at the condo daily and I called on a regular basis. But even that turned out to be a disaster. Sandie was no longer able to effectively deal with the facts or alter the situations she found herself in. Mom was neglecting Dad's care and her own care. Because of Mom's reputation for being in control and her constant reminders to us that she didn't need help, we assumed that she just needed little pep talks from time to time. But what she really needed was serious intervention.

I had for months been trying to convince Mom to send Dad to an adult daycare center in their community because I knew that it would give him the stimulation he needed and provide some oversight to his medical needs. It would also give Mom some much needed and well deserved time to herself.

Mom and Dad had visited my adult daycare center and loved it. They enjoyed the stories that I shared and marveled at how our guests (we called them "guests," not "clients.") not only maintained their independence but, in many cases, showed dramatic improvement in their cognitive, emotional and social skills. They plainly saw how families benefited from not worrying about the safety of their loved one during the day and how daycare afforded them some type of normalcy in their lives. Mom was amazed by the services we offered to our daycare guests and caregivers. She knew all of this from my years of sermonizing on the topic and now she got to see it first hand. Yet she remained reluctant to enroll Dad.

Mom needed desperately to get out from under the pressures and responsibilities of "24/7" caregiving. I tried to convince her that while Dad would be at the center she could once again become involved in the women's circle at their church, have lunch with her sister who lived in the same complex, go window shopping or experience the simple pleasure of getting her hair done without Dad tagging along. I saw the need for Mom to do something for herself, a notion she had long ago discarded as selfish and completely unnecessary. She needed to escape her reality and re-enter the real world. We urged her to attend support groups where she could share her caregiving stories, good and bad, with folks who had similar struggles in their lives. We thought she might find some peace in knowing that she was not on this journey alone.

After weeks of negotiating, choosing battles and doing my utmost to choose right timing (hostage negotiating would be easier!), I finally spoke as plainly and earnestly as I could.

"I don't understand why you are being so difficult! Why don't you want Dad to go?"

It was in that heated moment that the truth of the matter finally came forth. She replied, "Because no one can take care of your father like I can! And I don't want anyone to think that I can't take care of him any more!"

My heart sank – I truly felt deep sadness for Mom and I remember wanting to hug her. My heart said, "Do it." My friend, "Good Timing" said, "Not yet, Tom." You see, her first statement was true – No one could take care of Dad like Mom could. Even I believed that. If true love, loyalty and dedication are the measure of a good wife and a phenomenal caregiver, then no one could come within miles of Mom. But if Mom's first statement was true, then her second was the hard, bitter truth. It could kill Mom, literally and figuratively, if she believed that anyone thought that she could no longer care for Dad, or even worse, that she didn't have the desire to do so. Would people think that she was shirking the duties of a good wife? Would the "church ladies" judge her? Would her children and grandchildren think she had given up – that she was no longer in control? Worst of all, what would God think? My mom was not a "guilty Christian." She truly favored the notion of a loving, forgiving God – the New Testament God of covenant and promise as opposed to the Old Testament God of judgment and condemnation. But it always amazed me how, when it came to this topic, she lived in complete and total fear that God would judge her if she failed to see this thing through to the end. We grew up in a house where we were told to "never air your dirty laundry." Sending Dad to daycare was not just airing dirty laundry. No, this would be all out hanging wetted bed sheets out the window for all to see! What would the neighbors think when they saw the "school bus" arriving to pick Dad up? Surely they too would think she had given up and that she was sending her "problem" away to be someone else's problem for the day. And if they saw that, then surely they would see her coming home from a day at the beauty parlor and say to themselves, "Just look at her – she shipped the old man off to daycare so she could go and just have herself a day out on the town!" The mere thought of it all was more than Mom could bear.

"Mom," I quietly said, "You are so right. No one could ever take care of Daddy as well as you do. But the daycare staff knows that and they don't pretend that they can. Those folks are there to help you, not to replace you. Let's try adult daycare for a while, only three days to start and see how it goes. You're not locked into anything. If it doesn't work out . . . it doesn't work out."

After a full-term pregnant pause, she reluctantly agreed to allow Dad to attend.

"But only three days. And if he doesn't like it, he can stay home with me, and you and I will not have this conversation again!"

I smiled and nodded . . . and I gave her that hug.

The Red Foil Gift Bag

I wasted no time putting the ball in motion for Dad to begin attending adult daycare as soon as humanly possible. I was excited, to be sure. But deep down I knew that every minute wasted was one that Mom could use to back out of our agreement. As Sandie and I began to make the necessary arrangements we realized that any obstacle would give Mom the opportunity to renege.

Two items headed our list of possible negative issues that could easily turn into excuses: Transportation to and from the center and the costs associated with Dad's attendance. We selected a daycare center that had a great reputation and provided transportation. That took care of our first concern. I set out the next day to handle the second big hurdle, funding for Dad's tuition. Dad and Mom lived adequately on a small pension. I was sure that Dad would be eligible for the state Medicaid Waiver program that not only paid for a wide range of services but also covered the tuition and transportation costs. I called and scheduled an appointment at our local Medicaid office to determine Dad's eligibility.

About a week later Mom received a letter confirming her appointment accompanied by a list of materials and documents (read "red tape") that she would need to bring to that meeting. She called in a panic. She was feeling overwhelmed, inadequate to complete the process and frightened by her inexperience in dealing with a state agency.

"Not to worry Mom," I said. "Remember I'm going with you. I know exactly what they're going to want to see and I'll be over to help you gather everything."

That evening Mom and I went over the list and were able to get the requested documents ready for our meeting; utility bills, current bank statement, insurance policies and several others. How totally overwhelming the process is for the elder spouse who doesn't have anyone to assist him/her in preparing to seek eligibility from available funding sources. Still more daunting is the task of discovering what services are even available – only then can you actually "go shopping." Although the state system into which I was about to enroll my father is excellent, it could in no way be accused of being "caregiver friendly." It is intrusive, confusing and cumbersome to the very citizens it was designed to help. It carries with it the stigma that one is about to go on welfare and the misconception that recipients of such funding will ultimately lose all of their possessions including their home. Our seniors have worked their entire lives and have given money to the government to place into what I call an imaginary account. It is in times like these that they should be able to withdraw from that "account" in order to remain in their homes and continue to live as productively and independently as possible. As we all know, though, legislators and bureaucrats decide who gets that money and when. Unfortunately, the needs of our seniors often take a back seat to things like paving the highways and securing the nation. So seniors are constantly required to prove their worth and thus prove their worthiness to receive funding. To the extent that they are often perceived as no longer productive and a drain on the economy, the scales are weighted heavily against them and the uphill battle ensues.

That night I made a neat little pile of the information requested by Mom's case manager, placed a rubber band around it and slid it into a large envelope.

"Mom, just keep this on the dining room table until our appointment next week. This is all you're going to need."

The day arrived when Mom and I would venture to the Medicaid office to begin the process of determining Dad's eligibility to enroll in the program. Mom called me very early in the morning to let me know that she would be standing on her porch watching for me. To my astonishment and delight, there was an excitement in her voice that I had not heard for a very long time. As I drove onto their street I could see Mom patiently waiting on the porch just as she had promised. She looked beautiful! She had gotten her hair done just for this occasion and was dressed in her Sunday best, and I do mean best. She had decided to wear her favorite church dress. As she approached the car I saw that she was carrying a very large red foil gift bag. What in the world could that be? I got out of the car to assist Mom.

"Could you hold this for me while I get in the car?" she asked. And why did you bring the "soccer mom" van? You know I have trouble getting up into the seat."

Her anxiety was showing but it was almost nice to see her old opinionated self springing back to life!

As I hoisted Mom's four-foot nine-inch and, shall we say, substantial frame into the passenger seat of the van, I asked, "What's in the bag?"

"Well I thought that the more I brought to show the case manager the more she would understand that they have just got to approve Dad for the program. So I brought our bills, bank statements, and the mortgage contract for the condo and some other stuff from the last three years."

Her face was almost aglow with self satisfaction and confidence. I just smiled and said, "Good for you, Mom."

When we arrived at the offices I could see that Mom was very eager to get this entire matter over with. As I helped Mom out of the van, she sent out a general order, "Don't forget the bag, Tom."

I'm no fan of sarcasm, but the door had been left wide open.

"The bag?" I teased. Oh, you must mean the red foil gift bag that can be seen from outer space. You mean that one, Mom? How could I forget?"

As we walked into the building all eyes were fixed upon the four-foot nine-inch dynamo and her six foot son sporting his glamorous attaché. Hester Prynne had her scarlet "A" – I had my scarlet bag. Hester couldn't possibly have felt this self conscious! We signed in and were told to take a seat in the waiting room and that our case manager would see us shortly. There must have been seventy-five people waiting to see their case managers. As we walked in, Mom completely took the lead. It is said that there are those who "come to the meeting" and there are those who "enter the room." Romona Clark spent a lifetime entering the room (this was mostly a good thing)! With a walk of determination on this day, she didn't just take her seat as requested. Rather, she said "good morning" to everyone she passed. Those unwise enough to pause following the salutation found themselves a captive audience to Mom's "How I intend to get my husband approved for the Medicaid Waiver program in ten easy steps" monologue. Each would be sent away with her most earnest wish to "have a nice day!"

Now breathless from her gait and incisive talking, she motioned to me that there were two vacant chairs to her left. As she cascaded into one seat, she tapped on the seat next to her as a nonverbal cue that I was to sit there.

The room was bright with florescent ceiling lights. This created an immediate problem. The resonating light bounced off Mom's foil bag, creating a laser type beam that was shooting across the room and landing direct hits. The red beam of light found its mark on the face of anyone seated directly across from her. Within seconds of our sitting down, folks began moving to escape the intense red intruder. As the bag constantly slid off of Mom's short lap, no one was safe from the obnoxious light saber. People either moved or put sunglasses on to avoid going blind. Mom kept fiddling with the bag which caused the beam to be directed at innocents in every section of the waiting room. The more she moved, the more the light moved until absolutely no one was safe! Absent my degree in rocket science, even I could tell that the masses were becoming more than slightly annoyed with Mom. In an attempt to defuse what could have become an ugly scene, I tried to remove the reflective contraption from Mom. I suggested, "Mom, let's put your bag under my seat."

She replied with undying determination, "No, no, I'll just hold it. It's no problem. Besides, my entire life is in this bag and I don't want to let it out of my sight."

The light show continued for the next ten minutes. Soon the guards were coming into the waiting room to see what all the commotion was about. The clerks who were attending the registration windows were peering from the adjacent doors. My "patient son" act now nearing its conclusion, I firmly commanded, "Mom, give me that bag!"

Calmly grinning, she handed me the bag and said, "You're such a good son. It is getting pretty heavy."

I placed the bag quickly under my seat, abruptly ending the waiting room laser light spectacle.

Off To See The Wizard

No sooner had I secured the bag underneath my seat than our names were called. The door leading to the office pool of case managers opened and a shrill, over-worked and tense voice rang out, "Persons here representing Edward Clark please follow me."

Mom and I stood up. I felt like a character out of the Wizard of Oz. Every person in that waiting room was looking for something and all were confident that the Wizard would grant them everything on their wish list. We were about to follow the yellow brick road in search of the Wizard who could grant us funding. How exciting!

"Don't forget the bag," Mom reminded me.

As I retrieved the bag I suddenly noticed some apprehension on Mom's face. There was a look of fright and doubt. Her eyes fixed on me like a child looking for her security "blanky."

"Come on Mom," I said. "It'll be all right."

She smiled and indicated by her wide eyes and nearly blank expression that she wanted me to lead the way. I headed toward the waiting case manager with the red bag in tow.

As I arrived at the door I turned to hold the door for Mom and realized that she was thirty paces behind me. This woman, who just twenty minutes earlier had entered the room full steam ahead, was now terrified and unsure of herself. She was moving at a snail's pace.

The case manager who summoned us glared at me and said, "She'll have to move a little faster. We're on a very tight schedule." My heart sank with sadness at the total lack of compassion and concern for my elderly frightened mother that this state worker had just displayed. For the first time I realized that Mom was about to become just another appointment and number in a system that was overtaxed by the sheer number of people seeking assistance. I surmised from the case manager's tone that the system had done to her what it has and continues to do to so many of its workers. So many of them have become completely desensitized to the citizens, the people they were hired to assist.

"I'm sorry about your tight schedule but my mother is moving as fast as she can," I said apologetically.

Mom eventually reached the door. I smiled at her and told her in a soft reassuring voice, "Don't worry, Mom. Everything will be fine. I'm here to help you."

Mom smiled as we walked through the door. As we took our first step into a long hallway leading to the offices, the door slammed behind us and we both jumped.

"Looks like they need a new automatic closer on that thing," I kidded. We both chuckled. Our case manager never paused as she continued at warp speed down a long well lit aisle, all the while instructing us to follow her. As we walked down the hallway I could see over the numerous cubicles. The room looked like an enormous honeycomb. It was overwhelmingly huge. There must have been at least one-hundred cubicles set up like a labyrinth. As Mom and I were trying to take in our new environment, our case manager vanished. Where did she go? Which side entrance did she just escape through? How will we ever find her? Like a child who wanders from his parents at a department store, we felt a bit panicked. As we stopped to get our bearings we heard a faint, non-expressive voice urging, "This way. Keep going around the next corner."

As we rounded the designated corner, we found our case manager already seated behind her desk. At least I think it was a desk. The surface was covered by a massive, out of date computer, files stacked at least two feet high, and a phone which rang as we arrived and never stopped ringing during our appointment.

The case manager began, "Hi, I'm Ms. Brown and I'll be doing your intake evaluation for services today. If everything is approved I may or may not be your permanent case manager. We'll talk more about that later. Now I need to ask you some questions."

All of this was said without a breath and in the requisite rote monotone. Extending my hand I smiled and said, "Hi Ms. Brown. My name is Tom Begert-Clark and this is my mom, Romona Clark. We're here to see if my father might be eligible for the Medicaid Waiver program."

During this entire introduction Mom meekly hunkered behind me with only a portion of her red bag visible. Ms. Brown just stared at me.

I never stopped smiling nor did I retrieve my extended hand. Finally, Ms Brown shook my hand and said with a bit of hesitation in her voice, "It's nice to meet you. I'm sorry we're just so busy. Why don't you and your mom have a seat?"

I motioned for Mom to sit closest to the partitioned wall and I took the outside seat. I placed Mom's "life in a red foil bag" on the floor between us.

"Mrs. Clark, did you bring the items requested in the letter you received for Mr. Clark?" asked Ms. Brown.

To my recollection, this moment was the first in Mom's seventy-nine years at which she was unable to utter a single word. She just sat on the edge of the chair and stared at Ms. Brown, her face locked in an incoherent stare. Ms. Brown repeated, "Mrs. Clark, did you bring the items requested in the letter you received for Mr. Clark?"

The fear on Mom's face was indescribable. Even the beautiful makeup that she had so painstakingly applied that morning could not hide the fact that she had gone completely pale. She looked like she was applying for induction to Madame Tussaud's Wax Museum rather than financial assistance for Dad! Ms. Brown looked at me and said with little concern or emotion, "Does your mother have a hearing or language problem?"

Again speaking very softly, I addressed Ms. Brown, "No Ms. Brown, this is just the first time she has experienced anything like this and I'm sure she's just a bit frightened of you and this place."

This was the best substitute I could conjure up for what I *wanted* to say! In moments like these, I habitually recall the words of Psalm 141; "Lord, set a guard at my mouth – Keep watch at the gate of my lips." A side of me wanted to hurdle the makeshift desk and introduce myself more closely to Ms. Brown. My better and more intelligent side came rapidly to two conclusions. One – at my age, it's best to avoid hurdling anything. And two – we need something and the only thing standing between us and it is a stack of files and the lovely Ms. Brown, our "Wizard of Funding."

I reached over to Mom and said, "Mom, it's time to prove to Ms. Brown that Dad is eligible for the help we need. Let's show her what you've brought in the red bag."

I again offered Mom a reassuring smile. With all the gumption she could muster, she responded to me with a short, brief and strange looking smile. I picked up the red foil bag nestled between us and handed it to Mom. She took it slowly and then looked at Ms. Brown. With a wrestler's grip on the hemp handles of her bag, Romona Mae Clark sprung back to life – her previous bout with muteness proving short-lived!

"Ms. Brown I have taken care of my husband for nearly sixty years and I have never needed or asked for help from anyone. My husband and I are not educated people. I want you to know that. Because I may ask you questions that are dumb. I may not know how all of this works but what I do know is that we are good people. My husband worked hard his entire life. We raised three wonderful children and have several grandchildren. My husband has dementia. Tom tells me that Clark might get better if he can attend an adult daycare center. I want my husband to get better. I'm here to ask that you help my family make that happen. So yes, I did bring everything requested on that letter and more!"

And with that she tentatively rose from her seat, lifted her red foil bag over the top of the desk, and poured the entire contents onto the only remaining space at its center.

"I hope this is everything. My son is here to help me so if you have any questions, between the two of us, we'll answer them to the best of our ability."

She returned to her seat and restored her vice grip on the bag's handles.

I thought Ms. Brown might run screaming from her cubicle as her eyes fixed on the mountain of papers before her. She cleared her throat and began to slowly move all that Mom had deposited into a more manageable pile. I was so proud of Mom. I took her hand and whispered, "You done good, Mom."

"Why, it does looks like you have brought *everything* Mrs. Clark," Ms. Brown said sheepishly and with a hint of a smile.

In some strange way, I think Mom had just made Ms. Brown's day.

We remained with Ms. Brown for the next forty-five minutes as she entered information into her computer. After she entered a piece of information from a particular document, she would return the document to Mom. Mom would take it and lay it gently on the floor. Still nervous from her congressional address, she was clutching her red bag never thinking to simply return the documents to it. Then, without warning, Ms. Brown said,

"Okay, we're finished. Let me hit this last key and we should know if Mr. Clark has met all the requirements for eligibility."

Click, click, click (are those ruby red slippers I hear?).

"And he has. You'll be receiving your notification in the mail within the next two weeks. If you should have questions, please feel free to call me. Here's my card. Mrs. Clark, Mr. Begert-Clark, it was nice meeting you. Do you think you can find your way out?"

As if she had just ingested an illegal substance, Mom got another second wind and she immediately began speaking with great enthusiasm.

"Ms. Brown, it was a pleasure to meet you. You have been very kind. We'll just gather up our stuff and get out of your hair. My son has a great sense of direction and I'm sure he can get us out of here. Is there a restroom I might be able to use? I need to make a quick little stop. It's a bit of a ride home. You know how it is as we age . . . our bladders just don't hold what they used to!"

As Mom began this epilogue, I began to gather the documents from the floor and deposit them back into her red foil bag as quickly as possible. I finished my task just as Mom was completing hers. We stood together. This time Mom extended her hand to Ms. Brown, "It's been a pleasure. You just have a nice day!"

Ms. Brown did manage a smile and said, "Thank you both. It's been both a pleasure and an experience."

I smiled, "Mom, are you ready?"

"I sure am" she said. "And thanks again Ms. Brown. Oh, and by the way, lovely dress you're wearing."

"Come on, Mom," I urged. "I'm sure Ms. Brown has other clients to see."

As we searched to find our way out I looked at Mom and said, "I am so proud of you. You did this all by yourself."

Feeling her own sense of accomplishment, she gave me the biggest smile and followed it with her legendary hug and kiss. And then, the matter of funding now completely behind her, she asked urgently, "Honey, where did she say the bathrooms were?"

Warm Cookies For A New Friend

It had been about a week or so since Mom received her letter from the state notifying her that Dad was indeed eligible for services under the Medicaid Waiver Program. The letter explained that a waiver case manager would make a home visit to complete additional paperwork.

Mom called me on the phone.

"Tom, Joann is coming to make a home visit tomorrow. She's from the Medicaid program. Can you come over?"

"I sure can! This is exciting!"

"It sure is. I didn't unpack my stuff from our first meeting just in case someone else would want to see it. That was pretty smart thinking on my part, huh?"

"Sure was Mom, but Joann will only need to verify the information you gave to Ms. Brown and see what services you would like to set up for Dad."

Not hearing a word I had said, Mom excitedly continued, "I'll bake some cookies. Don't you think it would be nice to serve Joann some cookies and coffee? Or maybe she drinks tea. I have both. She was so nice on the phone."

"That would be lovely, Mom. I bet Joann would enjoy your homemade cookies. See you tomorrow."

As I walked into my parents' home I noticed that the person whom I supposed was Joann had already arrived and was seated at the dining room table.

"Oh Joann this is my son, Reverend Tom. He's going to help us do whatever it is that we need to do and he's been doing this kind of thing for years, working with seniors and all, so he's the expert so we should be able to get through all of this with no problem."

Mom said all of this without taking a single breath or losing her pasted smile. Joann and I exchanged a private smile, public pleasantries and proceeded to the task at hand. She said that her visit today was to determine whether this program was right for Dad and to see what help Mom might need with his ongoing care. Suddenly it occurred to me that Dad was not here with us. I asked Mom where he was.

"Oh honey, you know how nervous he gets over all this so I told him to take a nap. Do we need him? He really won't be able to answer Joann's questions anyway."

In bed? This news did not make me happy. Let's just put Dad to bed so we won't have to deal with him, I thought. Please, God, let the waiver program come through for Dad and get him out of that bed and away from Mom at least for a while during the day. Mom's crown was showing and, let there be no mistake, the matriarch was in control and would continue to make the decisions regarding Dad's care.

Joann urged us not to disturb Dad. She was confident that, between the three of us, we could answer the questions adequately. As Joann asked the first question, Mom interrupted, "Joann I baked some homemade cookies. When was the last time you had homemade cookies? I'll just put a plate out for us to nibble on while we're talking. Tea or coffee?"

Joann graciously smiled and said, "Coffee will be fine, Mrs. Clark."

"Call me Mona. All my friends do and I feel like we're already friends."

Mom was pouring it on thick but Joann was very professional and kind. For the remainder of the intake Joanna referred to Mom as Mona creating an open and stress-free atmosphere for our visit.

There were a ton of questions and again a review of the documentation Mom had presented at the Medicaid office. We gave Joann a detailed family history and Dad's medical information, including all of his numerous prescriptions and the names and phone numbers of his six physicians. After about ninety minutes the questioning ended and Joann asked what services Mom was interested in for Dad.

"Adult daycare only. Three days a week and if he doesn't like it Tom said he could stay home with me. Oh, and if you could get him a ride I would appreciate it. I could take him, but when I get behind the wheel of our car, Clark just gets all out of sorts."

"Mona, we can arrange for that and more," Joann replied.

"We don't need any other help, but thanks for asking," Mom countered abruptly.

Joann smiled as she looked at me.

"Well if you find in the future that you might, I can help you out. Okay then, we should be able to have Mr. Clark begin next Monday at daycare. Would that be alright?"

With that, Tom and Sandie's idea of daycare had just become Mom's reality. She replied as though panic stricken, "This Monday? Three days from today? I don't know if I can have him ready to go that soon."

I chimed in, "Joann, that will be fine." I turned and spoke to Mom. "Mom, there's really nothing to get ready. Dad will be fine."

Then to Joann, "Can we schedule Dad for Mondays, Wednesdays and Fridays with a pick up around 9:00 a.m. and a return home around 4:00 p.m.?"

"Sure. Have you picked out a daycare center?"

"Yes, the Antonine Sisters Adult Daycare Center."

"I'll give them a call and tell them to expect your dad on Monday. Mona, I'll call you to let you know everything is set."

Poor Mom! It was like she had been caught in an emotional tornado but had never heard the weather report warning of its coming. Never mind that we had been talking about this for weeks, right now the news was somehow sudden. I could see that this was all moving very quickly for her, but I had to seize the moment and make the decision now or she would never move to setting a final start date. Mom was overwhelmed. It saddened me to recognize the life changes which had taken place in my parents' home. But I needed to take control for the health and welfare of both of my parents. I needed to take responsibility to ensure that Dad would receive the best care possible and that Mom would begin to get some desperately needed rest. My emotions were mixed. I was happy that the decision had been made, but sad that I had had to so strongly influence it. Doing the right thing as an adult child isn't always easy. But seeing my parents slowly dying, figuratively and literally, was even more difficult. I had to look at this event as just one more part of my journey as a caregiver. I again turned to Joann.

"Thank you, Joann. Mom will be expecting your call. If you find that you need additional information please do not hesitate to call me as well. It's been a real pleasure meeting you and we look forward to working with you."

Joann sensed my Mom's dismay. She compassionately took Mom's hand.

"Mona, I'm not here to take anything away from you. I'm here to give you whatever you need to continue the special, loving care you have been giving Mr. Clark for over fifty-five years. I have several clients who are attending that particular adult daycare and they love it as do their caregivers. If you ever have a concern with the daycare or need anything, please call me."

Mom smiled and thanked Joann. But I saw something other than gratitude alone in Mom's eyes and her shallow smile. She was experiencing that horrible feeling of losing control and giving in. She was deferring to her children and the Antonine Sisters what she had so proudly done by herself for Dad over a lifetime. As we stood by the front door and waved goodbye to Joann, I gave Mom a squeeze and said, "Remember, no one will ever be able to care for Dad like you have. It's going to be okay, I promise."

Back to School at Seventy-Nine

The entire Clark clan was excited over the news that Dad would begin adult daycare on the following Monday. As it is our penchant for throwing a party for any reason, the family gathered on Sunday in preparation for Dad's first day at the center. We brought presents. A new pair of slacks, several shirts and pairs of socks and even tennis shoes. Dad was so excited. He proclaimed aloud, "Why, won't I look great my first day of school!" We all laughed, and from that moment on we all referred to Dad's days at the Antonine Sisters' Adult Daycare Center as "school."

Whatever it takes to have your loved one accept going to adult daycare, or to accept any decision you've had to make for their good, that's what you do. Some adult daycare participants think that they are going to work, to volunteer, or to school. Does it really matter how they refer to their day outings? It's all about care, stimulation, continuing to be as independent as possible and remaining where the caregiven wants to be – In his/her own home and in his/her own bed at night. This is how and where the caregiven feels safe and secure – in an environment with which s/he is familiar.

I called Mom before retiring for the evening on Sunday to remind her to have Dad ready Monday morning. Charlie, the center van driver, would arrive to get Dad around 8:30 a.m. There was some hesitation in her voice but she agreed.

"So Mom, what are you going to do tomorrow with Dad gone?"

"Oh I don't know yet. Something will come up."

That was "Momcode" for "I'm not leaving the house just in case the daycare calls and wants me to go pick up Dad." I gave no hint that I was on to her little plan.

Sandie, David and I were so excited and relieved that Dad would be participating in such a fine day program. We also felt that our decision would take away some of the pressure Mom had for so long experienced while caring for Dad. We hoped and prayed that they both would have physical, mental and spiritual healing in their lives.

It was 7:00 a.m. Monday when the phone rang. It was Mom.

"I got your father ready and he was so nervous that he had an accident."

"Is he alright? What happened?" I asked in a near panic.

"No Tom! He had an accident! He had to shower again and I had to change his clothes. I think he's not feeling well. I'm going to call the center and tell them not to pick him up today."

The adult daycare director inside of me flew into action.

"Oh, no you're not! You finish cleaning him up and have him ready when Charlie arrives. It's just first day jitters. It's just like when you sent me off to kindergarten that first day and I threw up! Did you let me stay home? Just to remind you, you washed my face and told me that I would be fine and out the door you sent me. I cried all the way to school."

"And I cried too!" Mom exclaimed.

"I didn't know that, Mom"

"Well, I didn't want you to see me cry. It would have just added fuel to the fire."

"Exactly right! Don't let Dad know that you're concerned, upset or worried. Clean him up and send him out the door!"

"Okay, but if he comes home and doesn't like the center he's not going back!"

"We'll try it for two weeks, Mom. Call me when he leaves."

At exactly 8:35 a.m. the phone rang. It was Mom and she was not of cheerful heart or voice.

"I hope you're happy. You're father is gone. You should have seen his face as he walked to the van. I thought he was going to cry. You and your bright ideas!"

"Mom, he'll be fine. You can call the center any time you want and see how he's doing. Try to enjoy your day. You need to get out of the house and go do something for you. Dad will be home around 4:00 p.m. Now go on! Have a fun day."

"Fine! Goodbye!"

Click . . . My mother had just hung up on me. She had never done that before. I kept thinking all day . . . "me and my bright ideas." All of the training, coaching and counseling I had given to dozens of others in this same situation could not have prepared me for this moment. It was amazing how I began to doubt whether our plan was a good one. I thought to myself, this had better work out or I'll never be able to get them help again, nor will I hear the end of it regarding this decision. Though it was never explicitly mentioned, Mom trusted me on this one. But now Dad's bodily functions were threatening to dismantle what I had worked very hard to build. I enjoy life and lament that time flies by so quickly. But on this particular day, I prayed for 4:00 p.m. to arrive in milliseconds!

I didn't hear from Mom the rest of the day but I certainly felt her presence with me. I knew what a difficult day this was going to be for her, but "tough love" made it all necessary. Imagine that; isn't tough love that thing that happens when parents won't let their twenty-something kid come back home because he's got issues that will only be resolved if he "gets out there and experiences the real world?" Who am I to play the "tough love" card on my own parents? To get through the day, I recounted in my mind – over and over again – the countless conversations I had had with other caregivers about those first days when their own loved ones boarded the vans to attend adult daycare. And I quickly remembered that fully 99% of those caregivers came quickly to know that it was the best thing they could have done for their loved ones and for themselves.

At exactly 4:10 p.m. the phone rang. It was Mom, of course, heralding Dad's return.

"Well, your father's home," she curtly announced.

By the tone of her voice, I was immediately convinced that it hadn't been a good day for either of them. I knew that I needed to ask how everything went and had made up my mind that, regardless of the answer, I would be understanding and encouraging, but firm and resolute regarding Wednesday's return. Bravely, I asked,

"So how did he like it?"

"I never left this condo. I stood by the window starting at 2:00 o'clock thinking they might bring him home early. The center never called me. And when he did come home, he jumped from the last step with a craft project he had done, a picture of him laughing and playing cards and a little report that says, "Eddy's First Day" which lists everything he did today. They call him Eddy! No one has ever called him anything but Clark! He had a wonderful day Tom, just wonderful! He said that he can't wait to go back on Wednesday. I hope you're happy!"

I hope you're happy? What the heck is that all about? Mom is upset that Dad had a good time? Quickly, I made sense of it all. She was upset that Dad had actually survived a day away from her and had had a good time to boot. She had hoped that he wouldn't want to return to the center ever again, thus giving her victory in the "who gets to care for Dad" sweepstakes. She feared his enthusiasm would tell the world that she had not been the best caregiver and that a "perfect stranger" was able to do the same and make Dad happy. What Mom did not realize is that she did make Dad happy. To borrow the cliché made famous by the fictional Jerry Maguire, my mom absolutely completed my dad. He loved her with all of his heart and soul. But no amount of encouraging could convince Mom that it was okay that she couldn't do crafts or play cards with him to keep him sharp and stimulated. The care she was providing was all about basic needs; bathing, eating, medicating. After that, she was too tired for "extracurriculars" (cuddling was definitely out of the question!). I suspected that Mom was actually feeling a bit envious, if not jealous. Dad had had a wonderful day. She had had a terrible day filled with stress and anxiety. This was not about Dad. This was a most rare and unflattering moment when it was "all about Mom." Realizing the dynamic – namely, that Mom was the one having trouble adjusting, not Dad – I played along and tried to turn the conversation into positive reinforcement for Mom.

"That's great Mom! Now on Wednesday you don't have to watch out the window or wait for the phone to ring. You can go have some fun. I'll bet it's a load off your mind that Dad had a good day!" Silence from the other end. Mom knew I wasn't giving in to the "I hope you're happy" comment. The truth is, I was happy and as time went on, she would be too.

Dad continued to attend on his appointed days and the change in him was remarkable. It was as if he had gone back in time. Joy and laughter had returned along with increasing self sufficiency and self confidence. He continued to get up at 5:00 a.m., but instead of escaping for a morning stroll, he showered, shaved and dressed himself. But Mom still struggled to appreciate these wonderful changes. Instead, she would chide him for getting up so early.

"Clark, the van won't be here for another three hours. Why don't you stay in bed longer?" she would bark.

Dad would persistently reply, "Oh honey, I don't want Charlie to have to wait on me. We have a lot of people to pick up on our way to school, you know."

Remarkable! Dear reader, did you catch that? He didn't want Charlie to have to wait. He *remembered* Charlie's name! Charlie was the center's van driver. He greeted Dad with a huge hello and smile. He always asked if Dad needed assistance getting in and out of the van. Of course, Dad would tell Charlie, "Oh thank you so much. I think I can do it. I don't want to be any trouble."

Charlie carried on light-hearted conversations with the participants as they traveled from one house to the next on his route. He talked about what activities would be taking place during the upcoming day and how much fun they would have. On the return trip home, he would ask about their day. There was always laughter and music in Charlie's van. Charlie had a passion and love for his passengers. Caregivers, when selecting an adult daycare center that will be providing transportation, always ask to meet the driver(s) who will be responsible for transporting your loved one. A good driver can make all the difference in the world. The tone for the entire day can be set by the driver who picks your loved one up in the morning and drops him/her off in the evening. Good drivers have even been known to gently persuade the caregiven on those difficult days when they would rather stay at home. They are vital front line staff and can be a caregiver's best friend.

A final word about Charlie. Of the dozens of people who filed through the receiving line at Dad's funeral, I don't know if anyone's presence there meant more to me than Charlie's. I may never see him again – I would not recognize him on the street today. But the image I have in my mind of the pure sadness on Charlie's face at the passing of my father is indelible. I shall never forget his presence and his purest expression of sympathy to me, Sandie and David. No small wonder that Dad enjoyed his ride to and from daycare as much, if not more, than his entire day at the center. Thank you, Charlie. And as "Eddy" would say, "Thank you so very much."

Mom's Black Wednesday

On the Wednesday of Dad's second "trial" week Mom received a call from the "Head Sister" at the center.

"Mrs. Clark, this is Sister Madeleine from the Antonine Sisters. Eddy has asked if he can begin attending five days a week beginning next week. If that's okay with you I can call Joann and get it set up."

In total shock and disbelief Mom respectfully responded. After all, she was speaking to a nun and the "head nun" to boot.

"Why, Sister Madeleine . . . uh . . . so nice to hear from you. So "Eddy" would like to increase his days? He never mentioned that to me but if that's what he would like to do, you have my permission."

The honey was dripping from her lips as generously as her sarcasm at calling Dad "Eddy."

"Oh I know this is a bit of a surprise. Eddy said he didn't say anything to you because he was afraid of hurting your feelings. He loves you so much. I told him not to worry because you would want him to enjoy the additional days with us."

Oh brother, Dad was going to get an earful when he got home that night! He had as much as promised Sister Madeleine that Mom would give him a hard time about wanting to attend five days. He all but admitted that he was afraid of her. Had he just committed the most mortal of Clark family sins? Had the dirty laundry just been hung out for all to see? Had poor, sweet Sister Madeliene unwittingly provoked war at the West Hampton Condominiums?

When Dad came home from school that evening, Mom greeted him with a painted smile and a cold hug.

"How was your day?" she asked in artificial sweetness.

"Oh honey, I had a great day. I played cards with the nicest people. And you won't believe it, but I danced with one of the sisters. I didn't know they danced!" he exclaimed in childlike amazement.

If Mom had recently been "on the edge," this comment sent her right over it! As Mom told the story to me several months later, she actually experienced some jealousy over Dad dancing and having a good time without her. Dear reader, understand that this reaction and these feelings are very common. Elder care professionals are keenly aware that their interaction with a participant can have such an effect on the participant's primary caregiver. If you ever have questions or concerns regarding the activities reported to you by your loved one, don't hesitate to call the center to ask or discuss. Like any worthwhile school or institution, the center should welcome your questions, comments and interaction.

Mom began to address Dad.

"Sister Madeleine called this afternoon to inform me that you want to go five days a week. I said that's fine."

Dad had not noticed the dagger headed straight for his heart as she continued, "If you would rather be with the nuns than with me, I'll survive!"

A direct hit! The battle was on. Score, Mona, 1 – "Eddy," 0!

Dad tried to defend, "Oh honey, you know that's not it at all. I love being with you. But they need me there to help. I set the table, fold towels, and talk with some of the guys who don't seem to be all with it. You know, that Alzheimer's thing is awful. Why, those sisters are the finest Catholics I ever met. Even though I'm not Catholic they ask if I want to go to morning Mass. And I go. We say prayers for people who come to school who might be in the hospital or sick. I say prayers for you. They are such good people."

"Mass!" Mom interrupted. "Are they trying to convert you? You remember that you are a ruling elder in the Presbyterian Church!"

"Oh honey, they don't care what church anyone goes to."

Then, without missing a beat, Dad concluded his "Top Ten Reasons For Going To School Five Days A Week" monologue saying, "Honey, you really don't need me here to help you. I just seem to get in your way."

Mom momentarily stared at Dad, digesting the truthfulness of his remark and asked, "What do you want for supper?"

Now, Sister Madeleine, the author wishes here to set the record straight on his mother's behalf. She loved you. She loved all of the sisters and direct care workers. Dad cherished his daily visits with Nurse Holly.

Mom and our entire family so appreciated the wonderful care extended to Dad. Mom's outburst was due, in large part, to her sudden realization that Dad was getting stronger and she was getting weaker. She feared that the day had arrived when her physical and emotional well was emptying faster than it could be filled. Although Mom never verbalized what was happening to or in her world, she knew in fact and faith that to all things there was a beginning and would be an end. She knew that nature was beginning to run its course in her body and in her spirit. Naturally, it scared her. We know that now. Because you are wise, you probably knew it then. Thank you, Sister Madeleine, and all of the Antonine Sisters, for loving and understanding Mom even when her behavior might have tempted you otherwise. Mom was a good person. We knew that. You assumed as much before you ever met her. Would that all of us would assume the goodness in others and operate on such a "wild" assumption. Thank you for your example. You have taught us well.

Why Don't We Sleep On It, Mom?

Dad always came home from daycare feeling tired but it was, as I've always referred to it, a "good" tired. He would return after his day at "school" and take a one-hour nap, eat supper, and be ready to visit the grandchildren, go for an evening stroll, or play cards. Mom could barely get his dinner ready before she was totally exhausted.

Dad was becoming more independent and Mom was traveling a path that was leading her to increasing dependence on others. She leaned more and more on my sister for nearly everything. My mother, once strong, bold, and in complete control, was nearing the end of her matriarchal reign. But even amidst her dwindling might and fortitude, she tried to resist the obvious; that she could no longer remain in control of her own life, let alone Dad's. She couldn't be Dad's sole caregiver much longer. Although this stark reality was ever before her, she felt as though she was being replaced and continued daily to engage in the battle to retain what little control she still had. Mom was losing the primary purpose of her life, caring for Dad.

It was at our family Christmas gathering in December, 2001 that Mom's declining health began to become so noticeable. She had not been sleeping and was unable to eat much more than a half slice of toast without escaping to the bathroom to vomit. These vomiting episodes had been a practically daily occurrence for months before we were made aware of them. Her olive complexion had taken on a pasty appearance that even her makeup could not hide. Her deep dark brown eyes had lost their luster and she had developed "raccoon eyes," enormous dark circles smothering the eyelids. Her weight loss was very apparent and, for the first time ever, we were telling her to eat whatever she wanted just to gain some weight. The only matriarchal trait that remained relatively in tact was the occasional (okay, slightly more than occasional) offering of her unsolicited opinions.

Sandie continued to beg Mom to go to the doctor to inquire if something could be done to make her feel better. A martyr to the end, Mom would try her best to reassure us that she was fine. In her mind, it just wasn't a convenient time for her to be ill. Who would take care of Dad? She would ride out the storm. She promised that if she wasn't feeling better in a few months she would make an appointment. Needless to say, we found this game plan totally unacceptable. In January our relentless nagging paid off when we issued Mom the ultimatum - Either you call for the appointment or one of us will do it for you. Mom replied quite predictably, "You kids are going to drive me crazy!"

Then a pregnant pause while she awaited the startling epiphany that we weren't giving in, "Alright, I'll call the doctor this week!"

Between scheduling difficulties with her doctor and her own "busy" schedule conflicts, "this week" turned into the beginning of March, but at least she had made the appointment. We thought that getting her to actually show up for it would be the next hurdle in the "Mona Marathon," but that difficulty never materialized. Sandie offered to accompany Mom and the offer was gladly accepted. Mom always felt more secure having Sandie, the family RN of whom she was so proud, with her. She was Mom's very own "private duty" nurse and walking medical reference library. But, of course, Sandie also had an ulterior motive; when the doctor asked Mom what was wrong, she would have to tell him, because if she didn't, "Nurse Ratched" surely would! With Sandie present, Mom could not try to convince the doctor that her children were just being overly protective and that she was "just fine." Now, I was generally the sneaky one when it came to action plans for my parents (see "cuddling" above – sneaky but not always successful), so this newly found penchant for stealth maneuvering on the part of my big sister made me particularly proud. As it turned out, neither Sandie nor Mom needed to do any talking. The doctor had plenty himself to say – there were definite and obvious problems.

Within just a few moments, the doctor discovered that Mom had developed a major problem with her esophagus and a hiatal hernia. She had suffered for years with this condition, but had been able to keep it largely under control through adjusted diet and medicine. But Mom had long ago given up the notion of "watching" her diet – it simply took too much effort. Further, Sandie and I had become convinced that she was not taking her medicine as prescribed. The doctor scheduled tests to be performed and set a follow up appointment for the next week.

Sandie again accompanied Mom for the tests and follow up. As they sat in the examining room, the doctor shared the results of the swallow test and showed Sandie the X-rays that had been taken.

"Mrs. Clark, what I'm showing your daughter is what your test results are telling us. Due to the history of your condition and the years you have been bothered by it, your X-ray shows me that the condition has significantly worsened. The only relief I can offer is for you to undergo a surgical procedure. It's a common procedure and the outcome for others who have had it done have been very good."

Amazingly Mom responded, "Let's get it scheduled as soon as possible. I can't stand feeling like this any more."

Sandie smiled at Mom and said, "Not so fast, Mom. Let's go home and discuss this before making a decision."

The doctor readily agreed, "In the meantime, Mrs. Clark, I want you on a puréed diet and you must drink at least one can of Ensure® daily. Stop at the desk and make an appointment for next week and we'll talk about your final decision."

None of us – Sandie, David or I – believed that Mom was strong enough to undergo a surgical procedure. But Mrs. Clark had another opinion and didn't care so much about ours on the matter. We wanted Mom to make an informed decision and so we pooled every piece of information, both good and bad, that we could find regarding the recommended surgery. But Mom never waivered from her original decision. We had done our best to present a fair argument. After a week of conversations and, having reviewed all of the documentation, Mom was all the more adamant in her desire to have the surgery. With nothing else to be discussed, we agreed to support Mom's decision and put our trust in her physician, her surgeon, and in her own history of strong will and incredible resolve.

Mom wanted the surgery to be scheduled as soon as possible. Sandie and I tried to convince her to wait until after October since my eldest son, Thom, was to be married in June and Sandie's daughter, Melissa, would be walking down the aisle in October. We scored a small victory when Mom compromisingly scheduled the surgery for June 10th, two days after Thom's wedding! Her own logic dictated that she would then be fully recovered in time for Melissa's wedding. Mom was planning her work and working her plan to be sure. Although we had our doubts, we supported Mom's decision and the schedule remained as she had set it.

The months leading up to Mom's surgery were anything but good. She continued to lose weight and was vomiting after any intake of food. Mom's daughter-in-law, Debi – my former wife and still very dear friend – gave her a small food processor so it would be easier to purée her food. Mom graciously accepted the gift but refused to use it.

"I'm not going to eat baby food!" she would complain to others.

When we would ask if she was drinking her Ensure®, her response was a resounding, "No! That's what they give sick people. I wish you kids would just stop worrying. Everything will be fine after the surgery."

Privately, Steve and I spoke often that if Mom remained on this course, she might not survive long enough to undergo surgery. In other private moments, we surmised that this surgery would either save her or kill her – there would be no "in-between." But publicly we stayed optimistic when talking with others regarding Mom's health. Sandie, for her part, began to make several trips a day to check on Mom. I could see and hear how tired and concerned Sandie was becoming. With each visit Mom would argue about any help or suggestion Sandie would make regarding increased food intake. We even started to entertain the possibility that Mom might need to have a feeding tube inserted. Our emotional roller coaster was perched atop the first and steepest hill and was about to take us on the ride of our lives. Medically speaking, the surgery did not kill Mom. Emotionally speaking, though, it proved to be the beginning of the end – June 10, 2002 would be the last day she spent in her own home.

Why didn't we take a more aggressive posture with Mom? Simply put, for all of the decisions regarding Dad for which she had "graciously" conceded and stepped aside, the decisions regarding her own health and future were clearly going to be hers and hers alone. A matriarch gets to do that. After all, she was the consummate caregiver – who could possibly know better? Sometimes I wish that we would have been more persistent. Most times, though, I accept the fact that we couldn't have been. The fact is, somewhere, deep down, we had to believe that Mom knew what she was doing. After all, even for all of her physical ailments, her mind seemed perfectly fine. She did not suffer dementia, she was well reasoned and very well planned. We reasoned that if she was able to take such out- standing care of others, surely she could and would take care of herself. Even though she was experiencing difficulties in some of Dad's care, he remained, due in no small part to her efforts, in good physical condition.

Like Mom, so many caregivers are so busy and consumed with their responsibilities that they often neglect their own health. Even though the caregiver is the one reminding the caregiven to take his/her medications, this does not imply that the caregiver will remember to take his/her own. Just because dinner is waiting on the table for the caregiven, it doesn't necessarily follow that the caregiver will partake. In so many cases, in the caregiver's mind, it is all about the caregiven and not about him/herself. Mom took this line of thinking to a whole new level.

Another thing that 20/20 hindsight has revealed is that we had all become so totally focused on getting Dad in to a healthy, safe, and home-like environment, that we may have neglected some of Mom's very basic needs. Dad was flourishing at the daycare. Mom, on the other hand, was melting away like a snowman at January thaw. Little by little, melting . . . bit by bit and day by day, dying. This is not to say that we "blame" ourselves for the way things played out. A hostage negotiator might have failed as miserably as we did at convincing Mom when she didn't want to be convinced. So we did what we thought was best once Mom made her decision about the surgery; loved her, supported her, and did our level best at creating an atmosphere that was positive and affirming. If we had to do it over again, would we have been more assertive, even aggressive in this and other situations, never minding the consequences, even when Mom insisted that everything was just fine? Would we have chosen to be right (is anyone ever?) instead of happy? I honestly don't know. We have poured over this, prayed over it, and debated it more times than I can remember. Some questions never get answered, I suppose. But one thing I do know is that regret, like anger, worry and countless others, is a crippling emotion and an incredible time waster. At the end of the day, when the roller coaster train returns to the station, if you can say without exception that you have done your best, then your sleeping will not be troubled. Though it's natural to do so, try hard to waste no time asking "What if?" or "Should we have?" or "Why did/didn't we?" Believe me when I tell you that you'll never get those questions answered to your satisfaction. Instead, spend that energy telling stories and recounting wonderful memories. Open that old photo album and remember all of the good reasons you had for doing what you did. Beating yourself up won't heal you – Picking yourself up will. Sleep well, good and faithful servant.

The Last Dance

The day had arrived for Thom and Cathy's wedding. June 8, 2002 was warm and sunny, a glorious afternoon perfectly fit for an outdoor wedding. For born 'n' bred Ohioans to make such brave plans is proof of their faith in a far greater power! Guests had begun to assemble in the small beautiful city park. Cream colored rented chairs placed in a semi-circle around a newly constructed gazebo were filled with family and friends. The gazebo overlooked a small placid lake where ducks were diving for their dinner. On the far side of the lake, a father and his small son stood fishing. The gazebo was just large enough to have the parents and grandparents seated within the structure so as not to miss one word or moment of Thom and Cathy's day.

Because I am an ordained minister, Thom and Cathy had asked me to officiate at their wedding. I was honored and thrilled to accept the invitation. At the time of my son's birth in 1977, I had not imagined playing this role in his wedding, but secretly I had hoped for it since my ordination in 1985. I don't know if a father, who just happens to also be an ordained minister, can experience a more blessed moment than officiating at his/her child's wedding. What a truly profound moment it was for me, and one that bore repeating. And so we did it all again in 2004 as my youngest son, Jason, married his dear Cyndi in June of that year.

Sandie and Bill arrived, with Mom and Dad in tow, shortly before the wedding was to begin. Dad looked dashing in his tuxedo, full of pride and excitement. He joked with family and friends that he was doing his best to avoid upstaging the groom in stunning good looks! Mom stood very still next to Sandie, clutching a small purse. Her dress was a soft flowing pattern in pink, her favorite color. She had made an early morning visit to her hairdresser. When the wind blew she would gently pat her hair to make sure it remained in place, never mind that hairspray had been applied by the beautician in tornado-resistant amounts.

As Mom and Dad prepared to be escorted to their seats of honor in the gazebo, I just stared at my parents and found myself pondering. What a loving and devoted couple they are. They had been good parents and I was grateful that they were here on this special day for their grandson's wedding. Then my thoughts turned from those of "father of the groom" to ones of "caring and concerned son." As I stood a short distance from my parents, I gazed upon Mom's face. I hardly recognized the once chubby, happy woman who had done so much for all of her children and grandchildren. She was thin and her face was drawn. Even the amount of makeup she wore could not hide the discoloration around her eyes nor lift her sunken cheeks. She was also sporting a nasty "shiner" to one eye, courtesy of a fall she had taken earlier in the week. She clung to Dad's arm with all the strength she could muster. What an incredible and uncomfortable irony; usually it was Dad clinging to her for safety and security. What had happened to Mom, the matriarch of our family, the sustaining pillar that would go to any length to keep her family together and well taken care of? The unstoppable march of time had taken us all beyond the mornings in which she had put socks on my feet before they ever touched the floor. The years had made the nimble antics of my youth on the freshly waxed wooden floors a distant memory. I swear that as the breeze gently swirled about that park, I could smell a faint scent of Clorox Bleach and Johnson's Paste Wax. As they moved so slowly toward the gazebo, accompanied by their grandsons, Jason and Shawn, I know that "Canon in D" was playing but all I could hear was Mom's silly morning song:

> "Good morning to you! Good morning to you!
> We're all in our places with bright shiny faces!
> Good morning to you . . ."

As my mind raced to revisit those memories, Thom placed his hand on my shoulder and asked, "Dad, are you alright?"

I turned and smiled, "Thom, I am more alright than you'll ever know. I am so proud of you. You are a blessing. Now, let's get this wedding show on the road."

And with a hug and a kiss, I led Thom, his brother, Jason, and his cousin, Shawn, to the gazebo. The closer we got to our appointed positions in the gazebo, I became overwhelmed with gratitude for all that my parents had given, shown and taught me. For the first time I was able to see all that my parents had given to me and what I had, in some small way, passed on to my sons.

The wedding went off without a hitch. It was at the final pronunciation, "You are husband and wife," that this ever calm, cool and collected pastor nearly performed "the ugly cry," but I recovered nicely. As Thom and Cathy left the gazebo I walked over to Mom and Dad and gave them a kiss and hug. They told me, as they had after every service since 1985 (somewhere near a million, I'm pretty sure!), "You did a fine job, honey."

And Mom continued, through tears of joy, "We're so proud of you."

After the photographer had finished taking family pictures in every imaginable combination and pose, the wedding party ventured to their cars for the short trip to the reception hall. We were ready for a party!

At the reception, Steve and I were seated at a beautifully set table with Mom, Dad, Sandie, Bill, and Steve's parents, Norm and Rita. Once everyone was seated, toasts were made, the food was blessed and the invited guests enjoyed a fabulous sit down dinner. As we enjoyed our meals, we shared in light conversation over the day's events thus far. I couldn't help but to continue my focus on Mom. I wish beyond wishing that I could sugar-coat it, but it is impossible; she looked purely awful and she barely said a word during the entire meal. As she sat among us, she busily rearranged the food that had been beautifully plated for her, never lifting a single bite of it to her mouth. I remember that she looked so small in her chair, barely able to sit up straight. What was most noticeable was her silence, something for which Mom had no prior reputation.

Following dinner the festivities continued. Cathy tossed her flowers, Thom shot the garter high into the air and the cake was cut. Now came the time we had all been waiting for . . . music and dancing. We had hired our good friend, "DJ Shelley," and oh what plans she had in store for our big bash! I don't remember the dance floor ever being empty the entire evening.   Even Dad was up on the floor as his granddaughters cajoled him to twist, waltz and circle dance. All the while, however, Mom just sat staring at the action with no expression on her face. "Mona" had come to the wedding, but Mom was nowhere to be found. A steady stream of family members and friends stopped by the table and inquired about her health. I heard her say repeatedly to her inquisitors, "After my surgery on Monday I'll be fine. Thanks for asking."

My heart was breaking as I watched this once social, vibrant woman remain seated to receive people. At past family celebrations, immediate family or cousins thrice removed it mattered not, she was the one moving table to table greeting the guests and making sure they didn't need anything. As bad as she looked, I can't help but wonder if some of the guests on this night might have known that it would be the last time they would see their dear friend.

At around 9:00 p.m. Sandie announced that she and Bill were going to take Mom and Dad home. Mom was tired. I expressed my sadness that Sandie and Bill had to leave so early but thanked them for taking care of Mom and Dad, especially on this night. As I moved toward the table to say good night to Mom, Shelley took notice and quickly but gently invited Mom and me to the dance floor. As I approached Mom I asked, "May I have this last dance of the evening with my mother? You danced with Daddy, so now it's my turn."

"Oh honey, I don't think I can. I'm a little weak in the knees," she said in a defeated tone.

"Not to worry. I'll hold you up!"

With that I walked Mom slowly to the dance floor. As I put my arm around her I could feel just how frail her body had become. I wrapped my arm around her and told her to hang on.

"Be careful with me, Tom" she said in a terrified whisper.

"You're in good hands, Mom. I'm not about to let anything happen to you."

I meant that on so many levels – I wished that I could protect her, that I could truly have the power to prevent anything from happening to her. But that's not reality and that non-reality was really beginning to sink in. It hurt more than anything had hurt in my first fifty years.

As we began to dance, Shelley announced, "Let me turn your attention to the dance floor as the Grandmother of the Groom, Mrs. Romona Clark, and her son, Reverend Tom, take a spin."

Everyone began to clap and whistle. I was so engrossed in the task of keeping a firm grip on Mom that today I can't remember the song we were dancing to. What I do painfully remember, though, is that I looked at Mom and smiled and thought that she surely would have gotten a kick out of all the attention being paid us. But there was nothing – absolutely, positively nothing in the face looking back at me. I wanted to cry. My good humor couldn't even fight this battle; it was under no compunction to lighten the moment, it had no urge toward any sarcastic comment about checking for a pulse. Nothing. I was going to have to "sit in" this one. Pretending to have no clue regarding the obvious, I asked, "Are you having a good time?"

Good Lord! Where did *that* come from? Flashback to the "cuddling" train wreck and it's going in the same direction, only faster! "How was your evening at the theater, Mrs. Lincoln?" might qualify as a less ridiculous question. With this one, I had surely made runner up. But Mom was always Mom – gracious, proud of her children, and playing pretend on their behalf on many occasions so that they would never suffer embarrassment. She dutifully replied, "Yes. I'm so proud of Thom and I just love Cathy."

I continued to look into Mom's drawn eyes and into a face that was so different from the one I knew. She never took her eyes off me. About half way through the song she said, "Okay, that's enough. Sandie's waiting to take Dad home. You know he's tired."

I kidded in reply, "Oh, and you're not? Are you going to stay with me then for the limbo contest? Don't worry, I'll take you home!"

"Oh, you know what I mean." she said with a small wavering smile.

"Mom, I love you."

"I love you too, honey."

We stopped dancing and I gingerly walked her to Sandie who was waiting near the door.

"Drive carefully," I said to her. "You've got precious cargo here, like Fred and Ginger, you know! I'll talk to you tomorrow. Love you."

Now clinging to one another just as they had toward the gazebo and had for fifty-four years prior, they moved toward the exit and into the beautiful June evening air. As I stood watching them leave, I felt like I was trapped in a slow motion scene of a movie.

> That's me on the dance floor . . .
> All alone on the dance floor . . .
> Just me . . .
> And a song I can't remember . . .
> Watching and wondering . . .
> Will I ever have this dance again?

Family Conference Room

Sandie had decided that while Mom was hospitalized Dad should stay with her and Bill. Since Sandie only lived a few blocks from Mom and Dad, Dad could continue to attend daycare and go to check on the condo whenever he liked. He was very receptive to the entire idea. Without any difficulties or hesitation, Sunday evening began what we all thought was to be a mini vacation. Dad and Sandie and Bill were really looking forward to this opportunity for "quality time" with one another.

It was 6:00 a.m. on June 10th when Sandie arrived at the hospital with Mom. With a small suitcase in tow, they checked in and began what would become a lost day for Mom and a long day in the family waiting room for Sandie. Mom was always comfortable having Sandie with her at the hospital, as were the rest of us. Her medical knowledge helped tremendously. Once the staff learned that Sandie was a registered nurse, they seemed more willing to share information that they had encoded on the "patient chart."

Mom's surgery was to have taken just under one hour. After three hours spent reading a very dated magazine from atop the waiting room coffee table, Sandie began to get a little anxious. Just as she was about to go to the patient information desk to inquire about the delay, she heard shouted from the desk, "The family for Mrs. Clark?"

Sandie approached the desk and was told to go to the family conference room where the doctor would be in to talk with her soon.

Family conference room? That had never happened before. Usually the doctor would come into the waiting room and give the brief and scant details regarding the surgery. Then he would tell us that Mom would be in recovery for about an hour. Next, he would urge us to go get something to eat and assure us that, by the time we had finished eating, Mom would be settled comfortably in her room and we could see her.

I had taken a few days off from work prior to Thom's wedding. I had told Mom that I wouldn't be able to be at the hospital during surgery but would come to see her immediately following work. Although Sandie understood my "dilemma," I knew that we had always done the "surgery thing" together and I thought that she might be feeling a slight sense of abandonment. Again with that pesky hindsight thing! I now remember the look on Mom's face when I told her that I wouldn't be there before she went into surgery. I had always been with her prior to her numerous surgeries. What was the difference this time? A little dash of "Professional Messiah Complex" anyone? I have plenty to go around. Why, if I missed an additional day of work, the company might fold! My 20/20 rear-view-mirror vision goggles have since revealed to me how ridiculous and selfish that decision was. But in everything we do or say, there can be a lesson. It only took me fifty years, but the one I learned that day – loud and clear – is that one about "family first." I forgave myself quickly for my error in judgment. And the simple reason for being able to do so is that my big sister forgave me *immediately.* Interesting how that works, isn't it? Thanks, dear Sister. If you didn't know how much that meant to me at that moment, you know it now. You've taught me many lessons in life, most all of them by loving example. When I grow up, I wanna be just like you.

As Sandie sat waiting for the doctor she felt uneasy and anxious. This was definitely uncharted water for her. The fear of the unknown can be awful. Soon the door opened. The surgeon sat in the barrel chair across from her. He wasted no time launching into his explanation.

"We ran into a lot of problems, Sandie. Your mother is full of scar tissue from previous surgeries. It took me a long time to try to remove as much as possible just to get to the acute problem. Once I got a look, I must tell you, I have never seen such a mess. The scar tissue had completely displaced your mom's stomach and it had attached itself to the lower part of her esophagus. It had been in that condition for such a long time that the majority of her stomach wasn't functioning and had become like leather. I had to reconstruct a smaller stomach from the little bit of good stomach remaining. After that I thought it best to get out of there and so I didn't do anything with the hernia. Actually, your mom can do fine with a smaller stomach. She'll just have to eat more often and in smaller quantities. I'm having her put in ICU for a while so that we can keep a closer eye on her."

My sister was totally taken back by what the doctor had just told her. "How long will Mom be in the hospital?" she asked. "When we spoke with you in your office you were talking about a few days."

"I'm looking at your mom remaining here for seven to ten days. It all depends on how well she responds to treatment. I'll stop in and see her this evening."

With that he stood up and shook my sister's hand.

"If you have any questions, give my office a call."

Sandie remained in the family conference room for a while longer just letting all that had been told her to sink in. As she replayed the conversation she looked around the pale blue room and overstuffed chairs. The inspirational pictures hanging on the walls didn't actually offer the inspiration she was seeking. Suddenly, as if a light bulb had just clicked on, she thought, "I have to call Tom."

Sandie lifted the receiver from the telephone that was sitting on a small end table next to the chair the doctor had occupied. Still reeling from the news delivered by the surgeon, she dialed nine and then my office phone number.

"When are you coming to the hospital?"

"I'm leaving work at 4:30. Why? How did Mom do?"

"Not good. At least I don't think she did well. They're placing her in ICU. So when you get here go directly to ICU. I'll meet you there."

I immediately left work and traveled the thirty minutes to the hospital. After parking the car, I don't remember my walk from the garage to the main entrance or my trip on the elevator to the third floor. The only thing that I recall is pushing the intercom outside ICU and telling the person who answered that I was there to see Mrs. Clark.

As the doors swung open I saw Sandie standing next to Mom's bed. I walked toward her and gave her a hug. She felt cold and the lack of color in her face was a dead giveaway for her fatigue and concern. Within minutes she gave me the doctor's report. I leaned over Mom, gave her a kiss and said, "Hi Mom. I'm here. Are you going to wake up to see me?"

Mom made a noise and opened her eyes slightly. Sounding like a drunk, she said, "Hi Tom. How was your day?"

She immediately fell back into a sound sleep.

Sandie and I had remained there for a few more hours when a nurse came in and told us that we would have to leave. We could see Mom again tomorrow during scheduled visiting hours. Hesitantly, we gave Mom a kiss and left her to the watchful and experienced care of the ICU staff.

Mom Has The Last Word

Recovery did not go well. Mom had terrible reactions to some of the pain medications being given her and she was refusing to eat. Factor in her body's routinely horrible reaction to any type of anesthesia, and you have a prescription for a very slow recovery. Those factors aside, her physician was at least pleased that the area of the surgery was healing nicely.

Mom remained in ICU for a week and was then transferred to a step down unit. There she continued her decline. Her list of refusals had by now expanded to include getting out of bed.

Mom's doctor had determined that the physical healing was actually progressing in a normal fashion. He believed that there were psychological issues impeding her progress. We asked for a psychological evaluation. This suggestion went over like a pregnant pole vaulter with the patient. No, Mom, we don't think you're crazy . . . we just want to *prove* it once and for all! Reluctantly, Mom agreed – she really didn't have much choice. The results indicated that Mom was suffering from post surgical depression.

As the days in the hospital lagged on, Mom exhibited very mean behavior toward Dad when he would visit her. There is no other way to describe it – mean is definitely the word. Interestingly, he was the only target. Others who came to see her were treated kindly and thanked profusely for their concern and for coming to visit. It wasn't a party, but Mom was at least kind and polite given the circumstances. But with Dad, it was a completely different story. She would keep her eyes closed while he tried to talk with her. If Dad would ask her something – anything at all – she would rudely snap a response. When Dad would try to encourage her to eat, she would tell him to mind his own business. Sandie and

I half-jokingly made a pact to ask the first nurse we saw, "Who is this woman and what have you done with our mother?"

After another five days, the doctors suggested that Mom be transferred to a floor that housed a new program specializing in delayed recoveries and issues of post surgical depression. While in this program, based in part on the principles and techniques of reality therapy, she would be required to get dressed each day, participate in physical therapy twice a day and go to a dining room for her meals. Mom could stay there for thirty days, but only if she showed some type of ongoing improvement.

After participating in the program for a week, nothing had changed. She took little, if any, food. She refused to get dressed, refused her therapy and would not even sit in a chair.

Places, everyone! Places! The "Good Cop, Bad Cop" show is about to begin!

Sandie would nightly do everything she knew to encourage Mom to "get with the program." Completely out of character, Sandie would often play "Bad Cop" and, if I do say so myself, she ought to have won an academy award. My sister doesn't have a mean bone in her body, but desperation can bring the Thespian out in all of us, I suppose. To be sure, Sandie was upset and, I dare say, even angry with Mom's behavior. We were fighting an uphill battle and getting no help from the woman in the bed with the anchor tied to her ankle!   In particular moments of exasperation, Sandie would switch on Bad Cop and say pretty much anything in an attempt to at least get Mom to fight again. She was "rewarded" with some pretty heated arguments and she easily became the new target of Mom's mean streak, but never did Bad Cop get what she wanted. She was hopelessly, helplessly stuck with an unwilling, unrelenting suspect who was defending her rights under some imaginary constitutional amendment. Mom wasn't saying it, but she was clearly communicating it – she had no further interest in living.   It is sadly proven, therefore, that great daughters make lousy Bad Cops.

Bad Cop having sailed off into the sunset, it was time for my starring role as "Good Cop." And what did I learn from this valuable experience? I learned that inside every Good Cop lies a piece of crap movie waiting to be summarily eviscerated by every "Roger Ebert" on the planet!

Good Cop tried to gently persuade the suspect that Bad Cop would "get off her back" if she would just eat a little or go to even just one of her therapy appointments. Suspect "doesn't care how much she rides me, I'm not hungry and I don't need therapy – I know how to walk!"

Score – Suspect, 1 – Good Cop, 0

So that she wouldn't starve to death, the hospital staff began to bring Mom's meals to her room since she would not join the other patients in the dining room. When her meals came, she would look at the full dish of food and complain, "I can't eat all that." She was right – She couldn't eat *all* of it. Instead she ate *none* of it. Not one morsel crossed her lips.

I brought a small bowl to the hospital from home and would meet the dietary staff in the hall. I would take a sampling of everything from the full plate and place the small portions in the bowl. The dietary staff would then take the nearly full plate into Mom. Together we would examine the meal.

"Mom, that is a lot of food but maybe you can eat this much."

I would then show her the bowl I had prepared.

"Well, I guess I can try it," she said, much to my amazement.

That trick, though, was short lived. Like a mother who laughs hysterically at her toddler's "knock-knock" jokes, I have come to believe that Mom was simply rewarding her little "magician" for his creativity. She "let the trick work" only one more time.

The frustration we were feeling over Mom's lack of cooperation, refusal of food and therapy, and her behavior toward Dad was beginning to take its toll on the entire family. To say that visits were "a little strained" is like saying that Hitler was "a little strong-willed."

One evening Sandie had brought Dad for a visit. Mom was so mean to him that he nearly began to cry. As Sandie and Dad prepared to leave, Dad gave Mom three kisses – it was always and forever three kisses. Sandie told him to wait in the hall because she needed to help Mom with something. The moment Dad was out of sight, Sandie addressed her mother and, this time, held nothing back.

"Mother, you are so mean to Dad! He loves you and wants you to come home. You are doing nothing to help yourself get better!"

With that, Mom displayed the first signs of life that any of us had seen in two months. Little did we know, however, that "Mount Saint Mona" simply lay dormant, awaiting the inevitable eruption that followed.

"The only reason you want me to get better is so that I can come home and take care of your father! And do you know what? I don't want to take care of him anymore! I don't want to take care of anyone! I don't even want to take care of me!"

By the end of it all, Mom was shouting. As Sandie stood with her eyes wide and her jaw tight, a pall of dead silence fell over the room. This gave Sandie some time. I know my sister. I'm certain that she wisely used it to pray and to ask God for the right words with which to respond. He gave me "cuddling" and "are you having a good time?" So much for the minister having that direct hotline that everyone thinks he has. To one who listens like I know Sandie does, he gave this – Sandie calmly but firmly looked at Mom and said, "Let me tell *you* something, Mother. From this day forward you will never have to take care of Daddy again. You decide if you're going to get better or not. But don't let Dad be a deciding factor. He is going to live with me."

She politely said good night and left the room. Okay, not much better than "Are you having a good time?" but surely better than I would have done. And in the end, had Mom recovered, Sandie surely would have taken care of *both* of them. Everyone, including Mom, knew that. Sandie and Bill had practically planned for the eventuality over the years. But Sandie needed for Mom to know, in no uncertain terms, that she simply would not permit Mom to cast Dad as the villain in this horribly sad drama which she had executively produced, directed, and was playing the lead.

Three or four days passed before Sandie returned for a visit. For at least that many days more, Sandie made excuses why Dad couldn't see Mom. After a week, the excuses ran out as did Sandie's anger with Mom. In all of the anger and shock of Mom's explosion a week earlier, there laid a very important and stark truth. Mom had cared for Dad for over thirty-five years and she couldn't and wouldn't do it any more. The caregiver in her was literally busted. Mom believed that if she returned home nothing would change and she would find herself back into the same old routine, the routine that was literally killing her. She could bear it no more. She had had enough.

Because of Mom's poor performance with her treatment schedule, she had to be discharged to a long term care facility. She was far too weak to come home and now required twenty-four hour care. We contacted our friend, Kathy, who was the Admissions Director/Social Worker at a wonderful smaller long term care facility. Kathy was able to get Mom transferred from the hospital to her facility in just one day.

As soon as Mom arrived she was treated like a queen. She was in a lovely private room with a private bath. The room had been freshly painted and bright curtains and a matching bedspread created a wonderful home-like environment. The room had a large window that overlooked a quaint side yard and allowed sunshine to flood her room in the early summer afternoons.

We thought this would act as a positive reinforcement and that Mom would snap out of her depression. Sadly, it did just the opposite. She continued her decline. Living solely on occasional sips of water, her major organs began to shut down. During visiting I would offer to help "freshen" Mom up. But the outstanding staff at the nursing home would graciously ask me to step out of Mom's room for a moment while they tended to her needs. They would remind me that her personal care was their job and that mine was to visit and encourage her.

I didn't think that was very fair. Their job seemed far easier.

Packing For The Trip

Steve and I were scheduled to leave for Boston to visit with some of his college classmates on Thursday August 8[th.] We were to return on Tuesday the 13[th.] At about 6:00 p.m. on the evening prior, I told Steve that I was going to take a break from packing and go to see Mom before we left.

"If you give me one minute, I'll go with you." Steve said.

I replied, "Thanks, honey, but I think I want to see Mom by myself tonight. Is that okay?"

Steve smiled, "Of course it is. I'll finish packing. Give Mom a kiss for me and tell her I'll bring her back some good tea from Boston."

Steve is a very intuitive person and he knew that I needed to spend some time privately with Mom.

Regarding Steve's offer to bring back Boston tea, I replied, "Oh that will be great! Mom's not giving everyone a hard enough time in her current mental state of mind. I can't imagine what damage she could inflict with a good caffeine buzz!"

Steve just laughed and gave me a hug.

"You drive carefully – I'll have everything packed when you get home."

As I walked into Mom's room, I had no idea what the day had brought upon her. The room was softly lit by a small light that was over her bed. The slightest scent from the flowers that the family had brought to her during the week graced the room. Cards, all expressing best wishes and containing messages of hope that she would return home soon, hung from the cork strip on the wall. The curtains that hung on the large window at the end of the room were closed so as to keep the darkness of night at bay. The bed linens appeared as they must have since early morning, a sure sign that Mom had barely moved during the day. Mom's breathing was almost undetectable as she lay so very still between the sheets and two white blankets.

I paused at the foot of her bed. Mom's pale complexion blended into the white bedding that was tucked underneath her chin – the best attempt by the nursing staff to stem her complaints of being cold. Her raccoon eyes looked even darker and larger than they had just the day before. Her lips, which just a few months before were full and colorful beneath her favorite lipstick, were peeling as a result of her refusal to take water or food. She looked so tiny in that hospital bed. I wanted to pick her up and hold her in my arms just as she had held me as a child.

I took a deep breath, walked quietly to the chair next to her bed, and sat down. It was a very comfortable and inviting chair but the mood in the room caused it to lose its intended appeal. Covered in a soft vinyl, we had draped a blanket over the back in hopes that when Mom sat there she wouldn't be chilled. In spite of our constant encouragement, Mom never felt the comfort of that chair. She refused to ever venture from her bed.

I gently and softly reached under the covers, being careful not to startle her awake, and took her hand.

"Mom, it's Tom. Are you going to wake up?"

She moved her small frail frame ever so slightly and turned her head toward my voice. She struggled a bit to open her eyes.

"Oh hi, Tom," she said without expression or seemingly any happiness that I was there.

"Hi Mom, how was your day?" I inquired, smiling.

There was no response. Just that same blank and eerie look to which we had sadly grown accustomed.

"Mom, I wanted to stop and see you before Steve and I left for Boston tomorrow. He said to tell you that he loves you. He's going to bring you back some Boston tea."

"Tell him I love him too," she slowly got out.

"Did you remember that we were going?" I quizzed her.

Again, no reaction.

I began to softly stroke the hand that I held so delicately within my own. I sat quietly, thinking that she just needed a little more time to wipe the sleep from her mind before talking to me. A few moments later I began again.

"Mom, do you want us to stay home? It's no big deal to postpone our trip to Boston until you're feeling better."

My question seemed to cause irritation and she looked surprised. She looked directly into my eyes and, in a weak but determined whisper, said,

"Absolutely not. You two go and have a good time."

Now this response was much more than the requisite, "Oh, don't be silly" or "Don't worry about me, I'll be fine" kind of comment that mothers and martyrs make when children ask if they should change their plans on their account. No, this was a calculated command to go – to go far away from here and to leave her be. It caused me to pause. I felt like she was practically ordering us to go. Why so adamant? Why so resolved? My pondering led me directly to the biggest and ugliest elephant that I have ever seen in the center of any room. The question begged and pleaded to be asked.

"Are you going to be here when we get back?"

Mom just continued to look at me. Again I asked, "Are you going to be here when we get back?"

Mom turned her head so that her eyes were fixed on the display of cards hanging on the wall across from the foot of her bed. She simply took a deep breath and shrugged her shoulders.

Oh, the irony of it all. Steve was at home packing for our trip. My mother had long ago finished packing and was ready for hers. My eyes welled up with tears. Inside, I was weeping from the moment I walked into the room. I knew in my heart that she had no intention of being here when we returned. I quickly prayed against it. Then, just as quickly, I realized that I couldn't pray against her. For all the permission that she had given her children over the years to do the things we wanted to do, go the places we wanted to go and, most importantly, to be who God created us to be, it was now my mother who needed permission to do what she wanted. She had never asked for permission before. Today, she was asking. With every ounce of conviction that I could muster, I slowly began,

"Mom, if you decide not to be here when we get back, it's okay. You are very tired and you need to rest. You have been a great Mom and I love you very much. We'll take good care of Dad. And don't worry about us, we'll be fine. Now, if you are here when we get back, I want you to forget all this mushy stuff!"

For the first time in recent memory, Mom actually chuckled. She then turned her head toward the wall opposite me. She squeezed her eyes shut very tightly. Over the weeks this had become "Mom-code" for "Visiting hours are over – it's time for you to leave."

I sat holding her hand for just a moment longer. Slowly I rose from my chair. My six foot frame towered over her bed. I looked down at my mother. I had an irrational urge to crawl into that bed with her and to simply, lovingly hold her – to do the same thing she had done for me when I was sick as a child. Where, in God's name, was that funny, hard working, opinionated, fat lady? What had happened to our matriarch who never doubted that she could do anything? It felt as if she was gone already – like she had already died. My spirit was bruised by disappointment, disbelief and, I can admit now, deep anger that Mom had given up and wanted to die.

I leaned over and kissed her forehead.

"I love you, Mom," I whispered into her ear as I gently laid my cheek next to hers.

A small, fading voice replied, "I love you too, Reverend Tom."

And that unforgettable "I'm so proud of you" smile made a final curtain call upon her tired, ashen face. Almost immediately she fell into the peaceful world she found in sleep.

I left her room slowly, quietly, pausing at the door for one more look, one last look. Sadly, this is one song I will always remember.

I remember thinking about Jesus when he was taken to see his friend, Lazarus, already dead three days by the time he arrived. From this moment in the Bible come three simple words that have, over a lifetime, given this pastor permission time and again to be human to his core. Those three simple words . . . "And Jesus wept." Having received my own permission, then, I stood alone in the doorway and began to cry.

Making A List And Checking It Twice

The grandchildren had begun to make their final pilgrimages throughout that week as well. Sandie and I were very honest with our children as to Mom's physical and mental condition. No surprises. It would have been totally unfair to have them walk into her room unprepared for what they would encounter.

Jason, our youngest son, visited Mom. Jason is our extrovert. He could make anyone laugh and especially his grandmother. Mom shared a special bond with each of her grandchildren, but there was something unique and special between her and Jason. She loved his spirit.

"Hi Gram, how's it going?" he asked.

His light natured self confidence filled Mom's room. Again, some come to the meeting. Our Jason enters the room! He parked himself right on the side of Mom's bed.

His grandmother spoke, "Hi Jason. Honey, I'm so tired. I have taken care of so many people. I enjoyed doing it but I don't want to do it any more. And, God forbid, I don't want anyone to take care of me. I'm ready to go Jason. I just want to go."

That special bond and understanding that Jason and Mom shared came immediately to the surface. His eyes welling up with tears, he put his hand on Mom's leg.

"Gram, I know all of that. So if you want to go it's okay with me. What great times we had, huh Gram? You spoiled me rotten! You have been the best Gram I could ever have. I'll be sad, but if that's what you want to do, I'm okay with it."

Mom smiled and closed her eyes. Jason said, "I'm going to go now, Gram, so you can get some rest. I love you." Jason stood and leaned over this woman who had, in fact, spoiled him as a toddler and protected him in his youth. In his early adulthood, Gram would, on a regular basis, re-mind him that he was to be a husband before he became a father!

"I love you Jason." she whispered.

Jason told me later that, although he was very sad, he felt special in knowing that Gram told him of her plans. He had a strange sense of self pride that he was able to let her go. I understand it now to be perhaps my son's first act of true selflessness.

As much as Jason is an extrovert, his elder brother, Thom, is the con-summate introvert. He is quiet and shy and struggles to express any out-ward emotion. He would have rather had all of his teeth pulled than to subject himself to visiting Mom in her current condition. Not that he loved his grandmother any less or differently than Jason or any of his cous-ins, but these were emotionally treacherous waters and ones that he would rather avoid. There always being strength in numbers, he loaded Cathy and their son, Andrew, into the car and they all went to see Grandma. As they walked into the nursing home, Cathy and Andrew headed directly down the hall to Mom's room. Ever conscious of protocol, Thom was the only family member to follow the facility's rules. He stopped at the front desk to sign in.

"Hey, you guys want to get Grandma in trouble or get us thrown out?" Thom called out to his scurrying family as he nervously scribbled his name on the guest registry.

In his best effort to break the ice and to calm his nerves, he sent An-drew into the room first.

"Great-Grandma, look who's here. It's me, Andrew!"

As Cathy and Thom paused just out of her sight, Mom opened her eyes. She greeted her great-grandson, "Oh Andrew, what a nice surprise! Where are your Mom and Dad?" That was Thom's cue that everything seemed to be alright and that it was safe to enter the room.

They visited for a short time. Mom was alert and able to carry on a good conversation. But any time the mood grew serious or heavy, Thom would have Andrew do something funny or sing a new song he had learned in pre-school. Classic Andrew "knock-knock" jokes also filled gaps in the conversation.

After their visit, their departure was as quick as their entrance had been. Andrew crawled onto the bed and gave Great-Grandma a kiss.

"I love you!"

Then he wiggled his way off of the bed and onto the floor. Cathy and Thom moved quickly to fetch their son who had fled the room, his mind set on exploring the remainder of the building. They spoke practically in unison, "We love you, Grandma. We have to go catch Andrew before he runs out of the building!"

Mom smiled and mustered, "Thanks for coming to see me Thom and Cathy."

The kids returned to the bedside for a quick kiss and then escaped into the hallway after Andrew.

As Thom walked down the hall he was overtaken with sadness. The tears that he had fought so hard to suppress began streaming down his cheeks. My son was heartbroken and his wife moved quickly to console him.

Sandie's son, Shawn – Mom's first grandson – and his gregarious wife, Stacey, visited Mom. Sandie's second born was the recipient of the best traits of both of his parents. Shawn is hardworking, handsome, a good husband and father and possesses an enormous loving heart. I had never seen Shawn as sad as he was during those last few months. Gram had been somewhat of a permanent fixture during Shawn's upbringing. She had spent many hours each week with him and his big sister, Melissa, when they were children.

The conversation during the visit surrounded the approaching arrival of Shawn and Stacey's first child, Joshua, due to the proud parents-to-be in January, 2003. The attempt was to steer the conversation away from talk of despair and imminent death. The kids did their best to keep the conversation upbeat by talking about new life, promise, futures, hopes and dreams. The kids thought that a little "reverse psychology" might do the trick. Sadly, even the magic that is the imminent birth of a child couldn't bring Mom around. Sensing that Gram was getting tired, Stacey announced, "Well, we had best be getting home. This fat mama needs to get some rest!"

Nodding in agreement, Shawn leaned over the bed to kiss Mom good-night.

"I love you, Gram" he said.

Mom replied, "I love you too, honey. You're such a good man. Take care of that baby."

If what you have read thus far in this chapter seems like a veritable checklist of visitors to Mom's bedside, then you are a perceptive reader. For, that's exactly how it felt and looked at the time and still feels today. Each visitor would today readily admit that when they paid the visits that you are reading about now, s/he knew then that it would be the final visit with Mom. It was as if Mom was simply checking names off a list as each child and grandchild made the compulsory pilgrimage to the nursing home. She truly did want to say goodbye to each of them; the loyalty and love of each visitor certainly simplified the task for the weary patient. As I began to hear stories about these visits, my mind wandered to imagine Mom taking a picture from each visitor and packing it in her suitcase – the one she planned to take with her to heaven – as she hastily readied herself for the trip. Once there, she would open the suitcase and show God, and anyone else who cared, the pictures of the family she held so dear. It would not stun her at all to hear God say, "Mona, I already know your children and grandchildren. I know each of them by name."

Undaunted, though, she would continue to show the pictures just in case even God had "missed something." Then my mind eased back into the stark reality of it all. On with the procession.

Mom had influenced all of her grandchildren, but perhaps none more than Sandie and Bill's daughter, Melissa. From the moment this first grandchild was born, Mom took special interest in Melissa. She seemed instantly to recognize that Melissa possessed all of the necessary qualities to become the next Clark family matriarch. Not a moment passed that didn't find Mom "grooming" Melissa and teaching her to be self expressive and bold in all that she did. In deep love and respect, I can honestly say that Mom accomplished her mission – Melissa is our family's "mini-Mom!" She has been blessed with the same determination, strong will and "whatever it takes" spirit. If opposites truly attract, then these two would have attracted one another something like oil and water. The battles began as early as when Melissa was just two years old. It was amazing to watch, really. The test of wills when Melissa wanted a sucker before dinner or refused to eat her green beans during dinner was something out of a university child psychology practicum course. Those battles, though the topics became many and varied through the years, continued to their last visit together.

Probably more than the other grandchildren, Melissa's sadness during that bleak July and August turned to anger. After all, her mentor had seemingly given up on life. Giving up was forbidden and had never even been addressed in matriarch prep-school. Melissa was unprepared and ill-equipped to deal with this new topic in the curriculum. But if true and abiding love means always being able to express oneself without fear of fracturing a relationship, then Melissa and her grandmother knew true and abiding love like none other. I don't know that anyone knew the heart and mind of Romona Baun Clark quite as well as Melissa did. And I don't know that anyone, save for Dad, loved or misses Mom more than she does.

Melissa and Kevin, her fiance' then and husband now, visited often during Mom's hospital and nursing home stays. Melissa was convinced that all Mom really needed was a kick in the butt to get over her current slump. Hers, of course, was the concern about her upcoming wedding. The deep bond they shared meant that four-hundred people could fill St. Michael's on October 26th but, for Melissa, that cavernous and beautiful building would be stone cold empty without Grandma there. No mincer of words, Melissa urged, "Gram, you better start eating and getting stronger because you are going to be at our wedding in October! And let me tell you, if you're not there I'm going to be very angry with you!"

Her grandmother simply unleashed a glance that seemed to tell Melissa, "I may be down but I am not out! I'll determine what I will and will not do. But . . . nice try. I'm very proud that you have learned your lessons well!"

Little did any of us know that Mom would indeed be at that wedding, not physically, but surely in spirit. You see, she had months earlier accomplished a very important task, one that absolutely had to be done before she went in for the surgery. Should a person undergoing surgery in early June have mended sufficiently to be able to shop for a wedding gift by late October? I'm no doctor, but the odds seemed pretty good to me. So why had Mom already purchased a shower and wedding gift for Melissa and Kevin and, in an attempt to conceal her post-surgical plans, already wrapped it and hidden it in her closet, only to be found at her passing? We have all come to believe the same answer to that question – Because it was part of the plan, that's why. And when Mom is making the plan, execution and follow-through are as good as guaranteed.

David's two daughters, Chris and Lori, stopped regularly after Mass to visit with Mom. She cherished them and their visits. David had divorced their mother, Diane, when the girls were just toddlers. But Mom had made it her personal mission to preserve their father's family ties. During those last months, Chris's and Lori's visits to Mom – as well as Diane's – were the greatest act of love they could have shown her.

Mom constantly taught – preached, practically – the lesson of "loyalty to family." She truly believed that her family was the most important thing she possessed, if one can "possess" such a thing. We were constantly urged to overlook the faults and failings of family members, even ones who had not been kind to Mom, for no other reason than that they were "family." We were told to forget about the past and to move on. When my marriage to Debi and David's to Diane ended, Mom was devastated. Indeed, she was sad to see those relationships ending (or at least dramatically changing) but she was even more fearful at the prospect of losing the relationship she had with her daughters . . . not daughters-in law, but daughters. That's how Mom viewed it – our wives were her daughters, period.

Not a problem. Mom would go to great lengths to include them in every family function. At first, it wasn't always the most comfortable situation, but it was Mom's situation – that's all that mattered. Mom continued to nurture her relationships with them. In the end, Debi and Diane knew they were Mom's daughters and they grieved as much as we at her passing. To this day, they attend many Clark family functions and what a blessing they both are!

On Debi's last visit with Mom, an honest, loving, and, as always, frank discussion took place. Debi's gift is the wisdom of acceptance. She may not always agree with you, but you will know when she has accepted you or your actions. She doesn't just tell you, "I accept that." No, Debi *shows* acceptance by her actions. This final visit would be a classic example.

"Mom, if you are ready to leave us it's okay. I love you. But Mom, you know that you can't go anywhere with your nails looking a mess like they do! Let me file and polish them for you."

Mom placed her right and then her left thin hand into Debi's. As Debi filed and polished, there was no further conversation. Just a loving, tender deed from someone who possesses the wisdom to accept a thing that she cannot change. For Mom's part, she knew that she needed to look her best, as she always did, when she traveled. Why should this trip be any different?

When Debi applied the final coat of pink polish to the last nail, she gently blew Mom's finger nails dry.

"They look great Mom. I think you're almost ready."

They exchanged smiles and a good night kiss.

Mom's list was winding down – Only three final visitors to see.

Checking Mom's Calendar

It was early afternoon on Saturday August 10th when Sandie asked Dad if he wanted to go see Mom. She and Bill had planned to stop on their way to go shopping.

What a ridiculous question!

"Honey, let me get my good shoes on and I'll be ready to go!" Dad exclaimed as he rose quickly from his recliner.

"Well if you're sure, Daddy," Sandie teased. "Take your time. We have all day."

Within five minutes Dad had his good shoes on and appeared in the kitchen.

"Come on. I'm ready. Bill, I'll sit in the back seat of the car so Sandie can sit up front with you."

Dad always sat in the back seat when both Sandie and Bill would travel anywhere with him. Always the perfect gentleman, it was his way of being polite. He never wanted to disrupt their lives or routine.

As they walked into Mom's room, she was sleeping. Dad walked quietly over to Mom's bedside and gave her his traditional three kisses on her forehead. She woke up and looked directly into Dad's smiling face.

"You scared me! At least you could have tried to wake me first," she scolded with a stern look on her face.

Sandie replied with just a hint of sarcasm, "Well, it's good to see you too, Mom. We thought we would stop before we went to the store. Do you need anything?" she asked, hoping to erase the disgusted look from Mom's face.

"No, I don't need a thing, but thank you," she replied, ditto the sarcasm.

What would prove to be Dad's last visit with Mom started on the downhill and continued its rapid descent from there. Mom refused to look at Dad. When he would ask her a question she would just look the other way, give a one or two word answer, or simply close her eyes to totally ignore him. She managed a lengthier response to Dad's inquiry about her lunch. Mom's tray remained, pristine and colorful, atop her bed table. Seeing it, Dad asked, "So, honey, did you eat something today? You know you need to eat so you can get better."

Mom stiffened her arms and hands to her side, glared straight ahead and sternly replied, "I don't want it. Why don't you eat it?"

And that was that – in any manner of speaking, the fat lady wasn't singing, but she was indeed warming up! Sandie and Bill had seen enough. The look on Dad's face could have pushed the coldest heart into automatic defrost. As tears began to well up in Dad's eyes, Sandie called an immediate halt to the visit.

"Okay, Dad, it's time to go. Mom's tired and we have to get to the store before it gets too late."

Dad hesitantly agreed and arose to bestow his three kisses.

"I love you, honey. I didn't mean to get you all upset. I'll see you tomorrow after church."

Her eyes closed once again and she squeaked out, "I love you too."

Attention, all rocket scientists, please report to the bedside of Romona Clark and explain what, in God's name, just happened here! We were baffled and we needed help. It didn't make sense – the meanness, the anger, the sarcasm – all of it directed like a precision missile at the man with whom she had spent the last fifty-seven years. Sadly, all rocket scientists were busy that day, and so we were left to dissect the matter for ourselves. In the days and weeks following Mom's death, we tried desperately to figure it all out. When a loved one dies, you spend time doing that. Like so much of life – and death – it has to make sense or we're not buying it. Our time spent analyzing that final visit has rendered this conclusion. The only person by whom Mom had yet to be granted permission to depart was her loving husband, her precious "Clark." That permission, the final go-ahead, would more likely be granted if Dad was so angry with her that he would welcome her absence. That sounds terrible and conniving, I know, but Mom desperately needed Dad's permission to fulfill her plan and would do most anything to get it. My heart has come to believe that she hoped that he would be glad to see the "mean lady" die. She also thought that leaving this way would make him stronger and more determined to live on without her. She hoped for an "I'll show her" reaction from Dad, an "I can live without you!" spirit that would signal the permission she sought. This contrived anger would also make things easier on her. If she began to pull away from him emotionally, it would make the decision to leave that much easier for her.

Allow me to explain it another way. Have you ever anguished over the decision to make a major purchase like a new car or even a new home? After months of discerning, you finally arrive at the decision to take the plunge. And in that instant, the car or home you own now, about which you have spoken so fondly and have called such a blessing for the last ten years, suddenly becomes a jalopy, a run down old shack. We can't say enough bad about it and we ramble on about all of the trouble it has caused over the years. Why do we do that? It's easy. We do it because we believe we need to justify our purchase, that we need some excuse for treating ourselves to something new. We want permission from our family and friends to go after what we really want. And we'll say anything – even things that aren't true – to win over the critics. This dynamic is consistently at work in the breakup of marriages or professional relationships. It's not enough for me to know that a new relationship or a new job is the best thing that could happen to me. Instead, I spend my time seeking the opinions of others, all the while steering the permission ship the way I need for it to go by saying every negative thing I can think of about that which I leave behind.

I have come to believe that Mom's situation was no different. It was just too difficult for her to simply say, "I'm tired – I want to go home." Though she had implied it to others, she just couldn't cross that line with Dad. And so she made herself believe, and did her best to convince Dad, that her body was a jalopy, that her home was a dilapidated ruins, that is was time to leave it all behind for something much better.

The author needs to be clear here – My mother did not commit suicide. People who commit that act do not seek permission. They generally act of their own accord and without warning. Some believe that suicide is the ultimate display of selfishness. I can only hope and pray that, as you have read my story, you have come to know my mother as anything but selfish. Mom was self*less*. The thought of deliberately leaving others behind – especially my father - to fend for themselves was not her modus operandi. I wish, of course, that she could have mustered up the courage to simply ask Dad if it was okay to leave. I know my father – he would have granted it in an instant. As we look back, it wasn't Mom's decision to leave that angered us. Rather, it was her treatment of Dad that made us angry and so very sad. But now that we think we understand it (will we ever totally understand?), our hearts are at peace and anger has been cast aside in favor of forgiveness. We have chosen to dwell on the wonderful memories of Mom and Dad's fifty-seven years together. Surely there is enough good there to outlast the sadness of their last fifty-seven seconds.

Caregivers, be vigilant and observant. Behavior like my mother's is very common (thank God, she turned out to be normal!). When one decides that "it's time," the attempt to cut the heartstrings that hold them back is painful to watch – more than you'll know until it happens to you. Be as understanding as your courage will allow. Be present. And, above all, be forgiving. Hopefully, reading my story and understanding the dynamic will allow you to be so as the scene plays out and not just after the stage is bare.

Bill kissed Mom. He and Dad headed into the hallway to wait for Sandie. By now, Sandie had become so accustomed to Mom's disagreeable and mean disposition that she had moved beyond scolding her. She had long since assumed the role of Dad's protector from the hurt inflicted upon him by Mom.

As Sandie straightened the bed linens around Mom, she asked, "So, are you going anywhere tonight?"

Faintly came the response, "No . . . not tonight."

I Did It My Way

On August 11th, Sandie, Bill and Dad left for Sunday school and worship at 9:30 a.m. They rarely missed either opportunity to visit this oasis of normalcy. They attended their church, not out of obligation, but out of love and faith. Church was as normal as breathing for them. With the world as they knew it seemingly falling apart, their weekly time in worship gave them an opportunity to recharge their batteries for the next round in the match called "life." There they walked, talked and worshipped with friends who had become a type of support group for their long journey.

Each Sunday while Mom was ill, the now inseparable trio would leave church and go directly to visit with Mom before going to a local restaurant for lunch. This Sunday was to be no exception.

As they approached Mom's room, the door was closed. Sandie surmised, "They must be changing Mom, Bill. Why don't you see if Dad needs to use the restroom."

As Dad and Bill headed for the restroom, Sandie stood outside Mom's room waiting for the staff to complete their task.

No sooner had Dad and Bill disappeared from Sandie's sight, than Mom's door slowly opened. The familiar nurse's aid nearly ran right into Sandie.

"Oh Sandie, I was just going to call you. We checked your mom at 11:00 a.m. and she was sleeping. When I made my next hourly rounds . . . she was gone . . . I'm so sorry."

Although this moment had been anticipated, the reality of the message and the sadness in the messenger's voice were still difficult to fathom. At a time when one's thoughts might race, Sandie's stood perfectly still, settling on one simple truth. Mom's plan had come to its successful and triumphant completion. Mom knew that David was in Atlanta, Steve and

I were in Boston, and that Sandie, Bill and Dad would be in Church. She had planned to make this last leg of the journey alone and she had worked the plan to perfection. She knew that there would be no one present to attempt to postpone the flight, nor anyone gazing pathetically upon her as she drew her last breath. No fuss would be made over this matriarch's abdication of the throne. After all, the transfer of power was meant to be peaceful, was it not?   And, most importantly, no one would witness her final moments and be tempted to view them as weakness. This simply would not be permitted.

As Sandie and I spoke later, we imagined aloud the scene in Mom's room as the hour approached for her to leave. While worship service was beginning, Mom was closing her suitcase.

"Hurry Mona, your aid will be checking on you," urged the voice for which she longed.

Sitting atop her overloaded suitcase filled with mementos of her life, she closed the clasps. She jumped back into bed like a child feigning sleep as her parents peek in to ensure that all is well. Then, as the first hymn was being sung at Wickliffe Presbyterian Church – the cue that the coast was clear – Mom grabbed her suitcase and made her escape for home, the place she longed to be.

The phrase "for heaven's sake" immediately came to my mind as Sandie relayed the day's events to me over the phone. I felt so sorry for the angels. God had created them to be servants to those whom He calls home to be with Him. Little did these worker bees know that there would soon be a new Queen Bee in town! I imagined Mom ordering those cute little-winged cupids to crawl under God's throne in search of dust bunnies. The vision of Mom's first stroll through the emerald grass that lines the streets of gold made me smile. She would never allow her feet to touch even one inch of those streets. Why, she might scuff them and, then, what? Her first question to anyone who even *looks* almighty –

"Can you tell me where I get some Clorox, some Johnson's Paste Wax, and a throw rug?"

The glorious reunion with her parents and others who had preceded her – an event about which she often spoke – and the calorie-less banquet that ensued must have been a sight! As guests arrived I could hear her yelling, "Be careful, I just polished the floors. I don't want anyone falling." The banquet, held in her honor, would be right up her alley. I could see Mom running around feverishly making sure everyone had plenty to eat and asking what else she might do to make their visit more enjoyable.

As a Christian, I believe that Jesus is sitting on the right hand of God the Father. As the son of Mona Clark, I believe that my mother is in the very next seat over, whispering her thoughts and opinions regarding the day to day operations of the mansion, into his ear.

During our phone call, I told Sandie that Steve and I would get the next flight home from Boston.

"Oh, Brother, don't do that," she lovingly suggested. "We have allot of out-of-town family coming in. They can't possibly get here before Wednesday. Just come home on Tuesday like you planned, but come straight to our house when you land, okay?"

Although Mom's family may not have been totally prepared for what had taken place, one thing was clear – Mom was. During the previous ten years, she had reminded us often that she had all of her wishes regarding her funeral written down. She continually told us, "When I die, go to the top drawer of my dresser and you'll find an envelope marked "Romona Mae Clark's Funeral Papers."

That notorious envelope. Five years prior to her death, the family had gone to Mom and Dad's for Sunday dinner. After the dishes were washed and put away, Mom disappeared for a few moments and returned with a legal sized envelope in hand. She asked Sandie and me to return to the dining room table.

"I want to show you my funeral papers."

Mom slowly opened the envelope that had yellowed from the countless times she must have removed and replaced the paper as each new wish and instruction came to her mind. She gingerly unfolded the contents of the envelope and laid it in front of Sandie and me to read.

Mom had listed the hymns she wanted sung and the Scriptures to be read. At the bottom of the information sheet were the words, "Presiding Clergy, Reverend Thomas E. Clark."

"Oh, terrific, Mom!" I shouted. "Be careful what you wish for. Do you really want me to have the last word at your funeral?"

Mom gave me that look that all parents have mastered and said, "Yes I do. I've told you on this paper everything I want done and you'll do it that way or I'll come back and haunt you!"

We all laughed. The prospect of it actually happening, though, ought to have terrified us more than it did.

That Mom had written these things down was no surprise, really. In every aspect of her life, she had controlled and directed her family so her funeral would, naturally, be no different. That she chose to reveal the information on this particular day was a mystery, but, nonetheless, Sandie and I promised, on the lives of our first born, (Sorry, Thom and Melissa!) to abide by her wishes and instructions. It seemed a wise thing to do.

Mom then carefully refolded the fragile paper and slid it back into the envelope. She pushed her chair back and requested that we follow her. She led us to her bedroom dresser and she opened the top drawer.

"Here's where you'll find everything we've discussed today. Don't forget where I have put this."

What Sandie and I had not totally realized until the Sunday afternoon of Mom's death, was what a great gift she had given us. We knew what her desires were for her funeral. It was clear and defined. There was no thinking, planning or discussion that needed to take place between Sandie, David or me. And most certainly, Mom did not want Dad to worry about any of the details himself.

Mom would remain in control even after her death. She didn't want anyone to ruin her farewell party and, heaven forbid, anyone would make decisions on her behalf when she would be unable to speak for herself. Even in death, Mom would remain her own primary caregiver.

Caregivers, as tough is it may be, spend the time now with the care-given, planning and preparing, so that you and others are not left to the task later. At a time when emotions are running at warp speed and stress is high, you'll be grateful that the logistics of the actual farewell have been planned, prayed upon, and agreed to in advance. Write it down and keep it in a safe place. You'll do a most wonderful and deserving honor to your loved one by eliminating fuss and fury when the event arrives.

Over the next few days Sandie and I phoned one another often. There were additional long distance conversations with the pastor at Wickliffe Presbyterian Church to make sure that she was comfortable with the additions to their traditional funeral service that Mom had requested. We placed several calls to our sons to be sure that they were okay and to assure them that we would be home soon.

Steve and I boarded our flight from Boston to Cleveland on Tuesday evening and arrived at Hopkins International Airport at 8:00 p.m. That flight was the longest flight I had ever endured. The ride to Sandie's home seemed equally long and was very quiet. Steve and I just pondered to ourselves our thoughts about Mom and our concerns for Dad. We were eager for all of the family to be together.

As we walked into the house, we were relieved to hear sounds of laughter and familiar voices. We knew by this that our family was doing well. We were greeted immediately by our sons.

"Dad, are you okay?" asked Jason.

I replied, "We're fine. How are you?"

Thom answered,

"We just can't believe that Grandma's gone."

We shared in a reassuring hug that made it clear that we were all on that same sad page. How many times had I been told by others that one is never ready, under any circumstances, to lose a loved one? How true those words rang in my heart and mind on this day.

My eyes immediately fell upon Dad as he walked, assisted by his cane, toward us.

"Oh hi, honey. How was trip? Can you believe how many people came in for Mom's funeral? She sure was loved."

"Yes she was. But how are you?" I asked as we embraced.

"Oh I already miss her, Tom. But you know she wouldn't eat. You have to eat to keep up your strength. There was nothing we could do. She's in heaven now. And I know she's happy. But I sure do miss her."

How fortunate we were to have had two towers of spiritual strength as our role models growing up. Dad had just lost his wife of fifty-seven years and yet he was able to find solace in his faith and the promised afterlife.

As I walked Dad to his chair in the family room, the house was alive with family from all over the country. As we passed through the kitchen, the dining table and every available counter space was filled with every kind of food imaginable. Neighbors, friends and parishioners had been so generous in their outpouring of sympathy as demonstrated by all of the goodies.

I turned to greet our relatives when my eyes met Sandie's. She is truly one of my greatest pillars of strength and my "bestest" friend. She walked over to me and joyfully announced to her company, "I haven't seen my brother in a week and we need to do some catching up."

She guided me through the crowd and into the bedroom that Dad had been using these past months. She closed the door and said very simply,

"Brother, I'm glad you're home."

Safely home now, in the arms of my big sister, the tears began to flow. Thank you for that moment, Sandie. You knew then, and you know still today, how much I needed that moment.

After a few minutes, we put ourselves back together again and I asked Sandie when David would be coming in. As it turned out, David could not get a flight out of Atlanta until Thursday morning. Bill would pick him up at the airport, bring him to the house for a quick freshen-up and then they would go directly to the calling hours.

Sandie wanted to talk for a moment about the funeral.

"Thomas, you know Mom's service Friday has got to be a celebration. No one can do that better than you can, Brother. It is going to be a celebration of life. We both know that Mom has received her heavenly reward. People need to see that we believe and know that the promise of eternal life is true."

Just who is the preacher here anyway? My sister can preach just as well as I can, to be sure. I seriously considered letting her *take* this gig.

I replied, "Not to worry, Sister! We'll have them on their feet praising God!"

We both smiled . . . and then more tears. These, though, were the joyful kind.

The Reunion

Steve and I arrived at the church for calling hours prior to the rest of our family. It had been nine days since I last saw Mom. I knew that her spirit was gone and that only her body remained, but I needed to see her. This was an important step as I began my own grief journey.

Steve and I walked into the narthex where the casket holding Mom's body was placed. It was surrounded by beautifully arranged baskets of flowers. I paused for some unexplained reason as I entered the room. I wasn't afraid to approach the casket, just a bit apprehensive.

"Are you okay, honey?" Steve compassionately inquired.

"I'm fine. Let's go see Mom."

Taking Steve's hand, we walked directly to the open casket which, of course, Mom had selected. It had a brushed silver exterior with a slight pink hue. A warm white blanket rested on Mom and her hands were folded in almost angelic repose.

The bright pink suit that Mom had selected brought back a flood of memories from her and Dad's fiftieth wedding anniversary celebration. Amazingly, it still fit her now diminished frame. Her hair brought a joyful remembrance of how she looked prior to her surgery. Her lips were full and vibrant with her favorite red lipstick. That's the way Mom always looked and that's the way she wanted everyone to remember her.

Even though she was gone, the look on her face spoke of royalty. I just couldn't get the thought out of my mind that the "Queen Mum" was gone now. "Her Majesty" had received a higher calling and was no longer available to her earthly subjects.

Sandie, Bill, David and Dad arrived shortly thereafter. Dad immediately walked up to Mom and, predictably, kissed her . . . three times.

"Honey, I love you," he said aloud.

David followed closely behind. As he approached the casket, he began to sob. My terribly sad brother had lost not only his mother but, as he and Mom often said, his best friend.

Mom and David shared a different mother-son relationship. Although there was always a parent/child respect, when Mom and David talked or visited one could sense that they were also very dear friends. Truthfully, their love for one another ascended to a plane that neither Sandie nor I experienced as children or adults. It wasn't "more" love or a "better" love – Mom was incapable of "playing favorites." It was just a different love, a unique bond.

Calling hours were to begin at 5:00 p.m. We all took our places in the formal receiving line and prepared ourselves to greet friends and family. Sandie and I flanked Dad, and David stood next to me.

People began to arrive before 5:00 p.m. and, by 7:00 p.m., visitors had been waiting in line for over an hour. As the flow of people seemed endless, I could see many of those who waited looking compassionately at Dad with unspoken concern that this might all be too much for him to endure.

At about 7:30 p.m., I asked Dad if he would like to sit down.

"Oh honey, I'm fine. The least I can do is to stand out of respect for all of these people who loved your mom."

Calling hours were to have ended at 8:00 p.m. At 9:30 p.m., the last caller left the church.

"Okay, Dad, I think we can go home now," Sandie said while holding his hand. "You've got to be tired."

"I am tired!" Dad said. "Let me just say good night to Mom before we leave."

Just as he had done every night before retiring, he kissed Mom three times on her forehead.

"I love you. Good night, honey."

He removed the handkerchief from his back pocket and wiped the tears from his eyes. He refolded it and returned it to his pocket and said, "I'm ready."

Without saying another word, we left the church.

I Can't Do This!

Friday August 16, 2002 was a very warm, sunny day. The temperature hovered near ninety degrees. The family returned to the church to greet more visitors for one hour before the funeral. Like a continuation of the previous evening, the line of well-wishers began to swell again. About ten minutes prior to the scheduled start of the funeral, people were asked to take their seats. Many of them did not get the opportunity to speak with us.

The immediate family was invited to extend their final goodbyes. What a sad but wonderful expression these final moments were. They offered a time of healing and at least some closure. One by one, Mom's grandchildren, accompanied by their families, gently placed their hands on Mom. Many offered a kiss as tears streamed down their cheeks. My heart was so moved as I watched our children – all grown up now with families of their own – embrace one another and offer other gestures of true support.

Now it was our turn – Mom's children, our spouses, and Dad. As we gathered around Dad to demonstrate our love and support for him, he did as he had always done. In grand silence, he gave her three final kisses and one last "I love you, honey." These could be heard throughout the narthex and those looking on listened to the sound of "Rosie John's" heart breaking. Following our farewells, all of the family members were escorted to the front pew in the church.

I remained with the casket not as the son, but as the pastor, just as I had done for hundreds of funerals prior. I asked the grandsons, who were to be the pall bearers, to wait in a connecting hallway for a moment. I would signal for them when we were ready to go into the sanctuary.

The funeral home staff slowly lowered the mattress that supported Mom's lifeless body. As they adjusted the pillow under her head, I chimed in, "Be sure to tuck that blanket under her chin. She's always cold."

Wow! Where did that come from? My faith told me that this was an empty shell, the simple physical remains of my deceased mother – Her spirit was long gone. But something in my flesh caused me to worry for her comfort. I realized the folly of my comment, but my human side would say it all over again if it had the chance. I have no regrets. The funeral director turned to look at me and I nodded my permission for them to close the casket. I retreated to the pastor's study to get into my clerical attire.

As I removed my alb from its hanger and placed my arms through the sleeves, I felt as though I was preparing to preside, as I did every week, for worship. I stood in front of a large mirror that hung on the back of the pastor's door and adjusted the robe. Next came my stole. Again I was feeling nothing out of the ordinary. All that was left was to put on my chasuble and Mom's "celebration of life" could begin. As I placed it over my head and gazed into the mirror, a vivid memory came upon me.

On the fifteenth anniversary of my ordination, the parishioners at All Saints Community Church in the small town of Cortland, Ohio, where I served as pastor from 1994 – 2004, held a special celebration in my honor. During the ceremony, I was called forward and asked to kneel at the foot of the altar. The leadership of our church came forward offering prayers and the laying on of hands. I was so moved and humbled by their gestures of faith, love, and support that I had not realized that they had returned to their seats and that Steve was the only person remaining on the altar. As I remained kneeling and offering my silent prayers, Steve tapped me on the shoulder and asked me to stand.

"Reverend Tom, in celebration and in honor of your fifteenth anniversary of ordination and as faithful servant to Christ's Church, the parish of All Saints Community Church would like to bestow upon you a special gift as a sign of our love and gratitude."

Steve moved to my left. As my body turned to follow him, I realized that Sandie, Bill, Mom and Dad were standing in the center aisle, each holding a corner of a beautiful cream colored chasuble that was decorated on the front and back with hand embroidered panels. The design is called "festive." The fine gold thread that had been woven throughout the panels reflected like rare gems in the sanctuary lighting.

Steve removed my green chasuble and my family came forward and placed this magnificent sacramental garment over my head. Each of my family members then greeted me.

"You are the best brother-in-law a guy could have," Bill said as he hugged me.

"Brother, you are truly a man of God – He's got great plans for your life," Sandie whispered into my ear as she embraced me.

Dad was next to offer his blessing with a hug and a kiss, saying simply but poignantly, "Oh honey, I love you."

Mom was last. The others had quietly and slowly approached me as they extended their kind and loving words. Not Mom! She ran to me. She nearly choked the wind out of me with her exuberant hug and kiss.

"Reverend Tom, I'm so proud of you. This robe is so fabulous. You'll have to wear it at my funeral!"

Those in the assembly who had heard her quietly laughed.

Wear it at your funeral? That was the furthest thing from my mind that day.

But today, as I vested for Mom's homecoming, it occurred to me that that day was today. The mere thought of it was deeply sobering.

My brief journey into remembrance was broken as the funeral director peeked his head into the door of the study.

"We're ready when you are, Pastor," he heeded.

I replied, "I'm ready."

But was I? Would I ever be *ready* for this moment?

As I prepared to leave the study, one of my dearest friends, Alice, was walking quickly past. Seeing me, she stopped.

"I'm sorry I'm late. I couldn't get out of the office," she said, catching her breath.

As she approached to embrace me, I looked into her eyes. At that moment, the humanity of Tom Begert-Clark scored a virtual TKO on the "divine" Reverend Tom and I began to sob.

"Ali, I can't do this! I don't think I can do this!"

I have never met that little guy named "Bejeezus," but I'm fairly certain that I scared him right out of Alice that day! Her eyes as wide as saucers, she placed her hands firmly on my shoulders and spoke gently, "Oh honey, yes you can. You'll be alright. I'll pray really hard."

She turned and rushed into the sanctuary. She turned again to take one last look at me before making the double doors and said, "You can do this!"

I took an incredibly deep breath and regained my composure. I motioned to the awaiting pall bearers that it was time for them to take their places along side the casket. As I watched them approach nervously and sadly, I smiled and said, "Gram would sure be proud of you all. You cleaned up real nice for her today!"

They laughed, and the tension of the moment was temporarily broken.

I turned and stood at the entrance of the sanctuary and joyfully announced,

"The peace of the Lord be with you!"

The response from the assembly – the same one I had heard hundreds of times previously – meant more to me today than it ever had before.

"And also with you!"

That simple phrase instantly brought the peace that I would need to be able to fulfill Mom's final wishes.

A Real VIP

Mom's celebration of life was exactly as she had planned. Brief moments of tears were drowned out by laughter as all bid farewell to Mom and celebrated her life. The uplifting music, lessons from scriptures, and homily recounted that Mom had led an amazing life and was now living her eternal reward. I shared the story of the chasuble and, at another point during the homily, I shared with the gathering the most important lesson that I had learned throughout this entire ordeal. During countless homilies over the years, I had urged my congregations, "The choice to follow Jesus is yours and yours alone. Even as your pastor, I cannot drag you, kicking and screaming, to Jesus or to heaven. You must make that choice on your own."

What I learned in the two months prior to Mom's death and shared with the faithful at her funeral was this:

"When someone is kicking and screaming to get *into* heaven – to go home – not even Reverend Tom can hold them back!"

To have said that was, I believe, a real moment of healing and understanding for me. I only hope that it was as much for my family and for all who gathered that day.

Immediately following the service, our family was escorted directly to a waiting limousine. Once there, Dad, Sandie and Bill, Steve and I, and David waited patiently for the throng of people to get into their cars for the procession to the cemetery.

The weather predictions for the day were correct. It was only noon and the temperature had already reached near the predicted ninety degrees.

"Mom can't complain that she's cold today . . . or can she?" I lightheartedly said, trying to break the silence in the car.

This was the first time in years that my siblings and I had all been together in one confined space with no escape route. As we shared our thoughts about the service, we remembered Mom's edict that family was more important than anything. We recalled the familiar mantra, "When you think you have lost everything you will always have your family."

Finally, the limousine driver arrived and commented to us, "We have never seen so many cars going to the cemetery. This is really something."

As we wound our way through back streets leading to the cemetery, we too were amazed at all of the cars. The line was so long that we couldn't see its end and, despite our futile attempts to do so, were unable to count cars.

Sandie spoke in amazement, "Oh my, when Mom would see this many cars in a funeral procession she would say, 'Someone really important must have died.'"

Without missing a beat, we all said in unison, "Someone really important did die."

Steve is so wise. He often tells me during times of difficult decisions, stressful situations, or moments of uncertainty, "Just sit in it."

By just "sitting in it," we will find the answers, receive the peace of understanding, and find the purpose of the experience. Each of us began to "just sit in it." We all remained completely silent for the remainder of our trip to the grave. At once, we were sitting in grief, disbelief, loneliness, remembrance, and, mostly, celebration.

The Voices In My Head?

By 10:00 a.m. on Sunday morning, the families who had traveled from across the country for Mom's funeral had left to return, leaving Sandie's home very quiet. Sandie, Bill and Dad skipped church that day so as not to rush the last visitor's departure. Sandie, the consummate hostess, sent each traveler off with breakfast and a blessing, "God bless you and thank you so much for coming. It meant so much to Dad and all of us. Drive carefully and call me when you get home."

Steve and I had gone to church to lead our community in worship and praise. That's what we do and that's what we needed to do. Although my heart was hurting from the previous week's events, I knew I needed to be surrounded by the love of my parishioners at All Saints.

After church, we came home, changed our clothes and went to Sandie's. Her living room looked and smelled like a flower shop, a vivid and colorful reminder that something very special had just taken place. But the kitchen looked ordinary again. The veritable buffet had been removed from the countertops and here, at least, life seemed normal again. We took our seats to have some lunch and began discussing how best to get Dad back into his normal routine.

"I think I'm going to have Dad attend daycare tomorrow," Sandie said. "What do you think?"

I quickly replied, "I think that's a great idea. Dad does so well with routine. And, if he stays home tomorrow, he'll just have time to relive his sadness."

We then shared "the plan" with Dad. After some slight hesitation, he too agreed that it was best to go. He missed his friends and the comfort and security that he felt at the daycare center.

"It'll be hard but I'll be okay," he said pensively. "Could you do me a favor, Sandie?"

"Sure, Daddy, what is it?"

"I know that they're going to ask me allot of questions. And you know my memory. Could you give me one of those papers to put in my wallet so that if I can't remember something, I could pull it out to get the answer?"

Deep sorrow came over his voice as he concluded, "I don't ever want to forget Mom."

He was referring, of course, to a copy of Mom's obituary. He was so afraid that, in the barrage of questions, he would forget something important to tell them. Sandie immediately retrieved a copy of the obituary and handed it to Dad. As if this slip of paper were something holy, he gently and lovingly folded it three times and slid it into the secret compartment of his wallet. We knew that this was special not only by his handling of it, but that it made the high honor of the "secret compartment" – that space previously reserved only for his stash of money and a picture of him and Mom.

At the crack of dawn on Monday, Dad was up and getting ready for his return to school. He seemed a bit nervous but was excited that he would again see his friends and the sisters. As the van pulled into Sandie's driveway, Dad asked if he could take one of the flower arrangements to the center. Sandie joyously replied, "Dad, you pick out any one you would like. I'm sure everyone would enjoy the fresh flowers."

He took but a moment to make his selection. Sandie carried the vase of flowers as she walked Dad to the van.

"Charlie, could you see that these flowers arrive safely to the center?" Charlie smiled and replied, "Sure enough! They are so beautiful. I know that everyone will enjoy them."

As Dad took his seat, Sandie moved to the front porch where she watched Charlie pull out of her driveway. As she waved goodbye, she suddenly knew how Mom had felt on Dad's original "first day of school." The memory warmed her heart and she headed back to the kitchen to try on a bit of normalcy for herself. A hot cup of tea and the devotional "Daily Guideposts" might just do the trick.

Dad returned to Sandie's at the regular time, 4:00 p.m. He looked tired but happy. He chattered excitedly, "Everyone was so glad to see me. No one really made a big deal out of why I was gone. All the sisters said they were glad to see me too and had been praying for me. I told them

I appreciated it. I think I'll lie down for a while. Will you call me when dinner is ready?"

Sandie was relieved that the decision to quickly get Dad back into the normal swing of things seemed to be the right one. She smiled, "That's a good idea, Daddy. You go lie down and I'll call you for dinner."

Caregiver, as difficult as it might be, it is important, even imperative, that the caregiven be allowed to jump back into the routine following any life-changing event. Whether it is the death of a spouse, a hospital stay, an accident or even just a family vacation, it is important that the "old habits" are given no chance to dissipate. Individuals suffering with dementia function far better by maintaining their day to day schedules. And remember, give up the guilt! Routine for them will also mean a return to routine for you – something you'll desperately need as you move forward in the caregiving journey. This is not the time to "sit in it." This is the time to get up and get going. You will have your moments, to be sure. But cease living *for* them. Rather, live *in* them as they come and move on from them as they pass.

As the week progressed, Dad began to come home with a strange and somewhat disturbing story. As Sandie inquired about Dad's day, he increasingly told her that he saw Mom going and coming from the daycare center. At first we thought that it was just a part of his grieving process. Sandie gently affirmed Dad's story.

"That's nice, Dad. Did she say anything to you?"

With a surprised and confused look on his face, Dad would simply reply, "No."

Wanting in no way to pry or to upset Dad, Sandie would tactfully change the subject. But this behavior continued for weeks, and Sandie and I became concerned. Was this all just a part of his grieving process or had he slipped into a "fantasy world?" We knew that it was not at all unusual for grieving individuals to have vivid dreams and to speak about their deceased loved ones as if they were still alive. Sometimes the behavior points to "unfinished business," or things they wish they had said but had left unsaid. A desire to continue the relationship that had been established for many, many years will often usher in feelings that the departed loved one really still exists and is making contact with them.

I encouraged Sandie to talk with Dad about his daily sightings of Mom, but to avoid any sort of reality therapy. Phrases like "You know Mom's dead," or "You know that she's in heaven and you'll see her some-day," might be perceived, even by the demented mind, as condescending statements of the obvious that could backfire. We both agreed that the events that Dad was describing were not scaring him. Instead, he seemed to be comforted by "seeing" Mom. Why, then, would we want to turn these seemingly happy sightings into something that would jeopardize Dad's peace of mind and joy?

The "Mom sightings" continued through September. Dad had a doctor's appointment and I suggested that Sandie inform the doctor and to get his opinion on the matter. As Dad sat on the edge of the examining table, and Sandie in a corner chair of the small examining room, the doctor very calmly asked Dad while checking his vitals, "So, Mr. Clark, how are you doing? I know you must still be sad over your wife's death."

Dad responded, "Doctor, I cannot tell you how sad I am. I miss her so very much. But she's in heaven. I'm living with Sandie and Bill now and I love it. I hope they do!"

The doctor continued, "You know, Mr. Clark, it is not unusual for people who lose a loved one after the number of years you and your wife were married to think they can hear their voice or maybe even see them."

"Really? That sounds kind of nuts!" Dad responded, as he wrinkled his forehead.

Sandie, having nearly fallen out of her chair at that last comment, said quickly, "Daddy, why don't you tell the doctor about your daily visits with Mom?"

With a puzzled look on his face Dad began, "Well, okay. You see, Doctor, each morning as I go to school I see my wife and then I get to see her on my way back to Sandie's."

"What do you talk about?" asked the doctor.

Now the puzzled look on Dad's face grew more intense. What would Dad say? Were the conversations and visits so personal that he would refuse to share them with the doctor? Would he break down as he spoke about his daily encounters? No, instead he would state the painfully obvious.

"Doctor, I mean no disrespect, but my wife is dead. She can't talk to me."

"Well what happens when you see her?" the doctor continued.

Dad now seemed increasingly perturbed with the interrogation. Sandie was just about to redirect the conversation when Dad took a deep breath and said, "Doctor, Charlie drives past the cemetery on the way to and from school. I can see my wife's grave from the van. I don't care what anyone thinks. I throw her three kisses and tell her that I love her and miss her. You don't think that's crazy, do you?"

The doctor smiled and turned his gaze toward Sandie. Sandie was red with embarrassment but, all the same, wanted to laugh or cry – she didn't know which – with relief. The doctor turned back to Dad and said, "No, Mr. Clark, that's not crazy at all. That's just a continuation of your and Mrs. Clark's love story. I think that's very nice."

"Well, I'm glad to hear that! Sandie has enough to worry about let alone having to worry about a crazy father!"

Sure enough, the route to and from the daycare center went past the cemetery. As Sandie and I laughed during the retelling of the story, I felt pretty silly that I had not looked at every possible angle, especially the daily route to the daycare center. Cross my heart, it never crossed my mind! Imagine that! Three weeks into the "grieving process" – that state of being that only the learned know anything about and are supposed to be able to expertly maneuver – and yet my father, the uneducated, blue collar farmer turned custodian, was light years ahead of the registered nurse and the licensed pastoral counselor! So much for the wisdom of books – I'll take Dad's kind any day.

Absence Makes the Mouth Grow Foolish

I think that caregiving is much like raising children. Both can be a formidable challenge. There are times that we may not like what our loved one is doing (whether in or out of his/her control), but we always love them.

I am a firm believer that situations are placed upon us for the purpose of strengthening us, not defeating us. But that little fella in the red suit with horns and a tail makes us want to sometimes forget the love part as we continue our caregiving journey. I continually told myself that caring for my parents had to be an act of love, not just an act of duty. In my mind, duty did not require an emotional response, but an act of love did.

Weekends with Dad were wonderful and pleasant. But when he came to stay with Steve and me for ten days, we found ourselves completely exhausted. To this day, I have no earthly idea how Sandie and Bill did it. "Raising" Dad turned out to be a full time job, never mind the fact that both of them had other full time jobs that actually paid!

I had committed to memory the "Keys to Caregiving." I use them in nearly every presentation I make to caregivers. Knowing those keys, I learned, is one thing. Applying them to my own life for those ten days was completely another. The keys are short and to the point:

- Ask for help
- Get support
- Change your habits
- Take a break

Yes, I would recite these daily, like an ostinato refrain in my head, during Dad's extended visits. But by the end of day six, my emotional car had two flat tires and one dead battery.

I know that providing care for an aging, ill parent or friend can bring out the best and worst in all areas of one's life, but never more strikingly than within the confines of sibling relationships. Ideally, the experience of caregiving is a time for siblings to come together and to provide mutual love and support. However, within a stressful transition like one parent's death, or in the day to day routine of taking care of someone, the pressure can also lead to strained family connections and painful conflicts. Invariably, the demands of caregiving can shine the light on old and sometimes even nasty habits and unresolved family issues. Past wounds are reopened and childhood rivalries reemerge. It is not unusual for adult children to find themselves replaying their historical roles in the family, recreating old dynamics of competition and resentment as they vie for their parents' attention and affection. All of this even when dementia has taken away our loved one's ability even to recognize who we are.

Yes, I knew all of that. I kept watch, stood guard, so that none of this would happen in *our* family. But all bets were off when my brother, David, would call long distance to check on Dad.

David had been living in Atlanta for several years, making only the rare pilgrimage to the old homestead and symbolic visits with the family. Why didn't he come to visit more often? Why didn't he invite Mom and Dad to visit at his home for a vacation? Why did his name come up every time we visited our parents as if he lived merely a block away?

Thanks! I'm over it. I'm back in control again! The answer is twofold and quite simple, really. David is the "baby of the family." And I suffer with the worst and most text-book case of "Middle Child Syndrome" known to psychology.

Following Mom's death, Sandie had disciplined herself to call David on a regular basis, generally weekly, to keep him informed about Dad. She made sure that David spoke by telephone to Dad whenever possible. I'm sure that this caused some discomfort in David as he emotionally wanted to "do his part," yet felt the pain of separation and distance that wouldn't allow him to do it. On rare occasions, David would call me and commence to an interrogation that would make any Spaniard proud. One after the other, he would fire questions at me regarding Dad's health and ongoing care. And one after the other, I would fire back answers – curt and short – as if English were new to me and I was as yet unable to form complete sentences in its use. I remember thinking aloud, after we had hung up, of course, "Could you really be that terribly concerned eight-hundred miles away?"

And then my mind would really start to race. Every time he called, I would emotionally drift onto the set of "The Brady Bunch." Marsha, Marsha, Marsha couldn't hold a candle to our David, David, David!

The stage for one such phone call was set when Dad was visiting with us for the weekend. We had planned a fun evening by inviting some of our friends, whose company Dad enjoyed, over for a backyard bonfire. As we prepared for the gathering, I realized that we had very little wood to support the main attraction. Steve made a call and found a place that sold wood by the piece. He and Dad set sail in Steve's car, lovingly referred to as our "soccer mom" van, and promised to return with enough wood to light up the night.

I was working in our backyard gardens when they returned. Like two exuberant hunters, they made their way up the driveway announcing their catch by endless horn honking. Dad was hanging out of the passenger's window smiling and waving – I wondered if his dementia had taken him on a private little trip to Macy's in November.

I had placed a lawn chair near the wood pile so that Dad could rest there while Steve and I unloaded the haul. I gave him a hand getting out of the van and directed him to the chair.

"Here Dad, you sit here while Steve and I stack the wood," I gently ordered.

May I just say, for the record, that if looks could kill, this book would have never been written. The author would have preceded his father in death. That look, oh, that look. It took me instantly back to my childhood. You know the one. When we were children, my father never spanked us. We didn't need it. "The look" was all that was necessary to open the tear ducts and right the wayward ship.

Dad reproved, "Tom, I've stacked more wood in my life than you ever will. Why don't *you* sit in that chair while Steve and I unload the van!"

Hesitantly, I caved in. I didn't think I had a choice, frankly. Too anxious to sit in the chair myself, I "allowed" Dad to help unload the wood, but I helped as well.

Needless to say, Dad was in his element. With his trusty dance part-ner, the name he had given to his cane, leaning against the backyard fence, he carried three and four split logs at a time. He never stopped carrying and never stopped talking. Instructions and nostalgic stories of his childhood filled the air. Steve and I became the audience for the lifetime documentary he was producing while stacking.

"Stack it cut side against cut side," he ordered. "This way it won't fall over. It leaves enough room for air to get through the wood to keep it dry and allow it to continue aging, you see. This wood is already aged and is going to make a great fire tonight!"

"You know, fellas, I was responsible for bringing split wood into the house for my mother. I would stack it next to the wood burning stove. The heat from that stove dried the wood even more. Mom sure could make some delicious dinners in that iron monster. The biscuits she would bake, oh the biscuits, they were as light as angel wings."

Dad stopped moving and stood very still, his arms filled with a few pieces of wood. He was going to a place far away and long ago and was taking us with him. His deep blue eyes glimmered as they filled with the fond memory he was about to reveal to us.

"Yep, as light as angel wings," he continued. "They had wings just like your grandma. She was an angel."

He paused again as Steve and I stood in stillness so as not to disturb his journey.

"She died of the cancer, you know. It was awful. She was such a pretty lady. She was a good mom. She worked hard raising us and taking care of Daddy. The life God had given her on that farm was terrible hard on her."

For a moment, Dad gently returned to the present, his eyes fixed on the two of us. The expression on our faces must have begged Dad to continue the journey.

"When I would finish stacking the wood next to Mother's stove, she would give me one of those hot, fresh biscuits right out of the oven. You know, we didn't have timers in those days – she just knew when the time was right. I think it was the smell, honey, that's how she must have known they was ready, you know. She had the longest fingers, you know, and she would pluck one of those golden beauties from that cast iron muffin pan. You'd swear it was alive, she handled it so carefully, you know, and then she would tear it in half and slather both sides with fresh churned butter and sometimes some of her homemade plum preserves."

He started to chuckle as he continued, "Mother would hand half to me as she held the other half for herself. She would say to me, 'We better have a taste. Now don't tell the others we had a bite. But I can't serve 'em for supper if they ain't good.' And she would give me a wink, you see. Man, fellas, that was some good eatin."

Dad closed his eyes. A great grin came across his face.

"I can still taste those biscuits!"

Steve and I stood in complete silence wishing to indulge our taste buds in one of Grandma's biscuits. It was amazing. I could, in some supernatural way, just feel that hot biscuit as the melted butter and warm plum preserves ran between my fingers. I had such a mind's-eye view of that biscuit in my hand, it took all I had not to raise my fingers to my mouth and begin licking each one so as not to miss one drop, one bite.

All three of us sighed, and, completely unaware of the impact this trip down memory lane had had on Steve and me, Dad looked at me and shouted,

"Hey, when does the help get fed around here?"

Moments after we finished "feeding the help" and sending him off for his afternoon nap, I returned to the backyard alone and I did sit in that chair and reflected on the event. Why had I been so resistant to allowing Dad to stack wood? Though age had slowed him considerably, he was completely capable of assisting. I know all of the rules about keeping the caregiven independent and physically active for as long as possible. Dad was, for the most part, still realistic and capable of making sound choices about what he could and could not physically accomplish. The answer came quickly to mind. It was fear. I had nearly allowed my own fear to influence my otherwise rational and permissive mind. And what was I afraid of? The answer to that is even simpler. I was scared to death that something would happen to Dad on *my* watch. It had nothing to do with Dad – it was all about me. If something were to happen to Dad while he was in my care, with what fury would I have to contend from my sister who trusted me, and my long distance brother to whom I felt no compunction to answer?

That evening, the invited guests gathered with us around a roaring campfire. Dad was so proud to tell them that he had stacked that wood by the fence, almost implying that he had preformed the task unassisted. He repeated his family remembrances of his days growing up on the farm. He never mentioned the biscuits, though. I think that was a once-in-a-lifetime moment between just me, my partner and my precious dad that I will cherish for a lifetime.

The following week, David called and talked with Dad. Again, Dad shared the story of stacking the wood during his visit with us. That little tidbit of information (Thanks, Dad!) precipitated a phone call from my brother. In hindsight, I should have taken the time to remind him that I was the ordained preacher, not he!

"Dad tells me you *made* him stack wood while he was staying with you guys last weekend. Tom, he's eighty years old and walks with a cane. I don't think that was such a good idea. He might have gotten hurt. Couldn't he have just watched? I can't believe you made him do that."

Now, when speaking with caregivers as they battle to keep their emotions in check with remote siblings, I always advise them that they should "express their feelings honestly and directly. Let the sibling know that you appreciate their concern, but that you have everything under control."

Dear reader, from the "do as I say, not as I do" department comes this stellar response from the author to his concerned little brother:

"Hmm, David, it's funny that Dad didn't mention to you that we *made* him rake the leaves, cut the grass, and take the trash to the curb! Give me a break, David! He just wanted to help! We kept a very close eye on him. He felt useful and the stories he shared were awesome. Not to worry. He had a safe and good time."

And then it happened. Apparently, my flesh hadn't had its fill, and soon followed the sarcasm. Before I could stop myself, I got downright ugly.

"You should have seen him, David. Oh . . . that's right . . . you live eight-hundred miles way . . . in Atlanta . . . Georgia! Sorry, I forgot – you can't see him from that far away, now, can you!"

Ever wish you could take something back, open your mouth and gobble up your own words? Only you know it's too late and the damage has been done? I thought to myself, "Oh, you handled that well, Mr. Professional Caregiver Advisor Guy."

When I came to my senses, which David has forgivingly assured me I did not wait too long to do, I realized that my anger was unwarranted and my sarcasm almost sinful. David was just showing his concern, and situations always look and sound worse to the person who is far away and hearing about events second hand. I reminded myself to whom I was speaking and heard my mother's voice just as sure as I'm writing this today, "Remember, when you think you've lost everything . . ."

Alright, alright! I took a deep breath, paused slightly, and then did something to my brother that, I admit, I have hated doing since the day he was born. I apologized to him. And, I dare say, I don't remember ever feeling better in the presence of or on the phone with my little brother than I did at that moment.

Caregivers, in order to survive caregiving, an occasional helping of one's own words and a side of humble pie will certainly appear on the menu. And where there are siblings involved, you'll probably need to take at least a few bites before you can move on to dessert. Exercise humility in your role. Remember, this is primarily about the caregiven, not about you. Understanding and accepting that very basic principle will help you tremendously as you deal with "sibling dynamic" issues that are sure to arise along the way.

And no matter how difficult it might be, do yourself a favor.

Call your brother.

He really does care.

It's A Normal Bodily Function…Really!

In my role as a pastor and, more recently, as an eldercare professional, promoting and protecting the dignity of all people, especially the elderly, has become one of my passions in life. Sometimes, though, the people who most crave dignity have as their fiercest enemy the uncontrollable march of time and its effect on their bodies. When the elderly caregiven begin to lose control of certain bodily functions, dignity can suffer a severe blow. It will be up to you, caregiver, to maintain it where you can and to restore it in moments when it seems lost. Above all – and here's the "advice" part of this and the next chapter – take what you do very seriously, but avoid, at all costs, taking *yourself* or your loved one too seriously. In the three-ring circus that is the loss of bodily function, go ahead and send in the clowns from time to time. You will need them to take the edge off. The bottom line is, sometimes you just have to laugh!

In case you are wondering, the answer is "Yes!" We are "going *there*."

If aging is all about "coming full circle," and role reversal is a hallmark of caregiving for the elderly, then it follows logically that our elderly caregiven may indeed journey back to childhood in the bodily functions department. Rookie caregiver, please allow us veterans of the game to introduce you to some of our very dear old friends. Over here we have our friend, the "incessant clicking of improperly fitted dentures." Next we have the lovely "involuntary tremor of most all useful limbs." To her left, please meet "irreverent burping." Across from him are seated the evil twins, "deafness" and "blindness." And last, but certainly not least, our constant companion, especially in restaurants, large gatherings in small rooms, and small gatherings in even smaller rooms, an equal opportunity invader happy to be here today – Say hello to the one and only, the ubiquitous, "Mr. Flatus!" If the Department of Homeland Security is still looking for weapons of mass destruction, it need look no further!

The "flatus phenomenon" in persons of advancing age or in those who are ill is quite normal. Someone, somewhere along the line, taught us that this was disgusting and repulsive. Children and the elderly remind us that it is natural. Admit it, you're laughing right now! In fact, you're laughing so hard, you probably just f . . . well, never mind.

Come on, let's face the facts. After all, it's "doctor recommended!" Have you ever had an abdominal or intestinal surgery of any kind? What's the first thing the nurse asks you after listening for "rumbles" in your stomach? That's right!

"Have you passed gas yet? You know, you can't go home until you do!" (Well, there is one more tiny little thing you must do, but we won't get into that.) The simple biological fact is that the digestive system slows down and can become quite finicky with aging. It can become over-worked just by the normal intake of food. Foods that were once gladly accepted are now rejected, some more severely than others. Add to the mix the stresses of aging and the plethora of vitamins and medications that are ingested and the stage is set for the eruption of "Mount Saint Flatus!"

In order to maintain or regain dignity in such instances, I have often found the injection of humor to be most helpful. One such setting for successful humor was, indeed, the hospital room of a patient from a church that I once served.

On more than one occasion while visiting parishioners in the hospital, the passing of gas became, if not the focal point of the visit, certainly the most memorable part of it. If the parishioner was alone in the room with me and the event occurred, I brushed it off without saying a word. Thus, dignity maintained and on with the visit. But if a family member of the patient was present, s/he would invariably succumb to the urge to comment, asking,

"Dad, did you have to do that in front of the pastor?"

On one occasion, someone in the room lost her dignity, but it wasn't the patient. His response to his daughter's similar question on that day was,

"What! I'm sure he does it too!"

The daughter wasn't laughing. The pastor was on the floor!

We all know that flatulent landings can leave behind a rather unpleasant fragrance. In the aftermath of one such attack on a hospital room, I was moved to one of the most creative and life-saving moments of my ministerial career. (Reader, please mention this to the beatification committee when my canonization is under consideration. I think you are required to have at least one healing miracle under your belt for consideration – what follows should qualify.) After the attack, there was no air moving in the room and what little breathable oxygen was left was being sucked up by the patient in the next bed (she lived, praise God!). I had the presence of mind to proclaim "Oh my goodness! There must be some evil spirits in this room. I'll get rid of them!"

I covered my mouth, staggered to the restroom, and retrieved a can of air freshener. In pastoral and ceremonious fashion, I waved the can in the air, spraying generously, praying profusely, and exhorting aloud, "Evil spirits, be gone!"

Soon, calmness befell the room and oxygen flowed freely once again. Gizmos and monitors hushed their beeping – the sound of unaided breathing could be heard anew. Reverend Tom had saved the day. But, wait! What is this? Why, some are still gasping for air. Oh, no! Is my work here incomplete? But, look again. What joy fills the land. The reason they can't breathe is because they're laughing too hard!

Yes, a little laughter can go a long way on this journey. Funny things will happen. The trick is to see them as funny as they're happening so that you can get the occasional respite that you deserve. Remember, caregiver, take what you do very seriously. But give yourself a break . . . and keep the air freshener handy!

Christmas Shopping With Evil Spirits

It was the early part of December, 2002 and we were approaching our first Christmas without Mom. Dad had transitioned well in making his permanent home with Sandie and Bill. Their devotion to his daily care meant that he was doing remarkably well.

As happy as Dad was, we all knew how much he still missed Mom. Nightly, before going to bed, Dad would ritually kiss his fingertips and gently transfer the kiss to an 8x10 picture of Mom that we had placed on his night stand. He would do this, of course, three times and follow it up with one "I love you." By now, he had added a new phrase to the routine.

"I miss you so very much."

He would then settle in for the night. I must admit, observing the ritual (he would also bring the picture with him on overnight visits to our home) would sometimes make the hair on my arm stand up. But it brought him much comfort. I believe that Dad knew, somewhere in his soul, that Mom could feel his kisses and know just how much he loved her.

I was scheduled to do an out of town presentation on the first Saturday of December. Steve offered that, since I was going to be gone for the better part of the day, he would call and see if Dad wanted to go to *Borders* to do a little Christmas shopping with him. Dad loved to read and loved a trip of this nature.

Steve is a wonderful caregiver. But he had never ventured for long with Dad by himself. Yes, they had gone to get ice cream and run to the local convenient store, but an entire day? I just wasn't sure.

"Are you sure you can do this? Can you handle Daddy by yourself?" I asked him. "Maybe you should wait until I get home this afternoon and we'll go together."

I didn't want to discourage Steve, but I wanted him to know that anything could happen and that he needed to be prepared. I look back now and realize that I must have sounded an awful lot like my mother. "Can anyone take care of Dad as well as I can?"

When Steve and Dad were together it was sometimes difficult to determine who was watching whom – they were like two kids and I know that *Borders* does stock candy!

Dad loved Steve. They shared the same sense of humor, faith, and love for music. Before Dad began to lose his hearing, he enjoyed listening to Steve singing and playing the piano at church and home. The two of them would engage in long conversations about everything from politics to religion to family issues. One of their favorite activities was to tease me mercilessly. There was no shortage of laughter when they engaged in this ritual activity.

I always thought that there was an overwhelming possibility that my father – and even my mother - loved Steve more than he loved me! But I learned to deal with my insecurity in a dignified and mature manner. If it seemed that Steve was getting all of the attention, I would simply assume the "sad position" – shoulders slumped, arms hanging limply at my sides, face frowned, head bowed down and audible sigh. Invariably, someone would say,

"Ah, we love you too, Tom."

All better now.

I will never forget the occasion on which Dad said to me, privately,

"Tom, Steve is one of the finest men I know. What a blessing he is to me and how lucky you are to have him share in your life."

Quick! Run to the kitchen and bring the entire box of tissues – I'm about to do the "ugly cry!" I always knew that Dad felt this way about Steve and our life together, but for him to have said it proved to be a most tender and memorable moment.

As I prepared to leave the house and Steve prepared to pick up Dad, I felt the caregiver compulsion to present him with a lovely detailed listing of "dos and don'ts" for their little day trip.

- Remember, no milk products
- Morning meds are 11:00 a.m. Don't forget blue plastic pill box

- If going to lunch, stay away from fried foods and salads. Sandie & Bill will know if you mess this one up, believe me!

- Walk slower and park as close to entrances as possible.

- Keep an eye on Dad. *You* behave!

After a quick review of the list, Steve graciously and respectfully smiled and said, "We'll be fine. If anything happens, I'll have Dad call your cell phone from the police department!"

As Dad and Steve pulled out of Sandie's driveway, Steve asked Dad what he thought might be the perfect Christmas gift for Sandie and Bill. Steve knew what his response would be and Dad did not disappoint. Without a moment's hesitation, Dad said, "I bet we could find something at *Borders!*"

With that, "my boys" set sail. As they arrived inside the store, both headed directly to the religion section, hoping to find the latest devotional guide. After looking through the selections for about ten minutes, Dad looked at Steve and announced that he needed to make a visit to the restroom.

Steve immediately replaced the book on the shelf and proceeded directly toward the appointed destination. As was often the case when "the urge" hit, Dad became a little impatient. He began to discuss aloud – very aloud – his recent problems regarding the "natural bodily function" discussed a chapter ago! To add insult to injury, the progression of Dad's disease had rendered him nearly deaf, and so he seldom realized how loudly he was speaking. He was a librarian's nightmare.

As they walked through the store toward Dad's second-favorite room (the bedroom had become his favorite – the place where he would go to "just rest his eyes" after dinner), he began speaking in a tone more suitable for the playground than a bookstore.

He said to Steve, "You know, honey, I think it is all this medicine I'm taking that gives me this terrible gas!"

Steve could see a few of the other patrons take leave of their reading material to glance toward him and Dad instead. Unwittingly, Dad continued right along, "I try to control myself, but sometimes I can't."

Now the faces of the onlookers turned fearful. Could this handsome, white- haired, blue-eyed octagenarian really do them any harm? Dad's "clincher" would answer that question and send them reeling for the exits, sans cappuchino . . .

"And when that happens, Steve, I feel sorry for anyone that's within ten feet of me. Honey, it's like something died inside me!"

As they got closer to the restroom Dad became disoriented and thought that he had lost his way. Now my father knew the directions to every restroom in every building that he might possibly be in. The shortest distance between two points is not a straight line. It's the path to the restroom taken by my father, period! Ask any mathematician who has followed him there. But today, for some reason, he felt lost. As the matter was, in his mind, urgent, he asked a rather attractive young woman (he always had an eye for beauty) if she might know the way.

"Excuse me, honey, but it is very important that I find the restroom before the evil spirits are released. Do you happen to know where the restrooms are?"

One of the things that caregivers, my own family included, must learn is to always expect the unexpected. We learned quickly to simply build a bridge across any embarrassing or shocking situation and to cross over it. This, though, was a veritable drawbridge and it was up! No crossing allowed. My poor Steven had absolutely nowhere to go.

The young woman looked surprised, but was very kind.

"It's about two aisles straight ahead."

Then she did the sweetest thing. She leaned in toward Dad, put her hand on his shoulder, and said, "Not to worry, sweetie. You'll make it."

Dad was always demonstrative. He gave the young woman a gentle hug and said, "Oh, thank you, honey."

As she walked away, Dad turned to Steve and said, "She was very nice. But you know I can't hear a thing . . . What did she say?"

By the time Steve had replayed the young lady's conversation for Dad, they had reached their destination. Steve waited anxiously outside the door for what seemed like an eternity. Finally, after about ten minutes (a long time in restroom-speak), Steve went in to check on him. He called aloud, "Dad, are you alright in there?"

To which came the simple yet maddening reply, "Well, I *thought* I had to go . . ."

Later that evening, while sharing the story with me, Steve and I laughed until we cried. It was funny, to be sure. But, if memory serves me, I don't recall Steve ever again taking Dad on any day trips by himself.

Incidentally, he completely missed those 11:00 a.m. meds, and, not amazingly, they never did get lunch.

A Place I've Been Before

To say that things were going well would be a total understatement. Dad's health seemed to be better than it had been in years, thanks to Sandie's constant attention to his medications and doctor appointments. Between Sandie and the nurse at the daycare center, any changes in Dad's physical or mental health were noted and the appropriate actions taken immediately.

Things were going beautifully . . . but beauty is fleeting. Dad began to have episodes that were short in duration but mirrored symptoms of a stroke. He would become disoriented, his complexion became ashen and clammy, he was unable to speak clearly and his coordination was shaky at best. Immediately after each episode, Sandie would take his vitals but they remained nearly normal. Following the episodes, Dad would become very tired and would require days to recover. As time went on, the episodes became severe.

On the first such occasion, Dad was up early on a Monday morning getting ready for daycare. He was attempting to clean the blades of his electric razor when one of the rotary blade guards fell into the drain of the sink. Dad always felt, and went to great lengths to announce, that his presence at Sandie and Bill's must be a horrible burden on them. He had grown to despise the fact that he needed the care and attention that he did. He made constant apologies for the attention paid him and felt that he could never do enough to "repay" their sacrifice. The razor incident proved to be the eruption point for months of pent up emotions, particularly anger. Dad was enraged with himself for being so "stupid" as to let the blade fall into the drain. He was convinced that a plumber would need to be called in and this only added to his frustration. He worked himself into such frenzy, that he became completely incoherent and could not respond at all to Sandie when she discovered him. Sandie took his vitals and surmised that he may have suffered a stroke. An ambulance was called immediately and he was taken to the emergency room. Bill placed a frantic call to my office to alert me. I told him that I would leave my office immediately and meet them at the hospital.

The drive from my office in Canton to the hospital in Youngstown normally took around ninety minutes. On this occasion, I'm sure I made it in much less time but it seemed like an eternity. As I drove, my mind was reviewing Dad's health history. There was no history of stroke on Dad's side of the family. He had a normal blood pressure (or so I thought); in fact, it sometimes ran low. He maintained a low sodium diet and didn't smoke. Again came the questions. What could it possibly be?

As I rushed into the hospital, I was directed to where Dad was awaiting tests. I pulled the curtain open to find him sitting upright on the gurney.

"Oh hi, Tom," he said. "Honey, I'm sorry you had to leave work. I don't know what happened."

Sandie and Bill were sitting next to Dad with a look of total bewilderment on their faces. Sandie said, "Bill, stay with Dad a minute and I'll fill Tom in out in the hallway."

Sandie retold the events leading up to that point.

"Tom, by the time they got Dad here, he was coming out of it. No one seems to know what happened. I'm thinking that Dad will be released shortly."

But that wasn't to be. About an hour later Dad's attending physician came in.

"After conferring with your dad's primary physician, we have decided to admit him and run some further tests."

We felt good about the decision but Dad did not.

"I want to go home! I'm fine."

"Dad, it looks like it might be a day or two. It's better that we try to find out what happened by admitting you now. Hopefully they'll find something out so this doesn't keep happening," Sandie explained.

Dad hesitantly agreed. As we accompanied Dad to a regular room he looked at me and said quietly, "Tom, take me home . . . please?"

The look of panic and fear on his face nearly broke my heart.

"Dad, I'll tell you what. If they can't find anything in a few days I'll take you home. Is that a deal?"

"Two days and that's it!" he stated.

Without realizing it, I had made a promise to Dad that I had no idea if I could fulfill. If only I had known then what I know now, I would have never uttered those words.

As it turned out, I was able to keep that promise (as if I had any say in the matter). Dad was released three days later but, in spite of all the testing, the culprit remained on the loose. We were simply told to keep a close eye on him and to call again if there were further episodes.

Only three days later, another seemingly more serious episode occurred. Sandie discovered Dad sitting in his easy chair in the living room in what can only be described as a catatonic state. He was motionless, speechless, and seemingly lifeless. Sandie managed to arouse him from his stupor just enough to know that he was at least alive. She took his vitals and, based on his incredibly high blood pressure, made the decision to return him to the emergency room. She surmised that, if he hadn't already suffered a stroke, he was at least in grave danger of suffering one soon. This time she and Bill drove him to the hospital despite his pleas to turn the car around, go home and just try to "let him sleep it off."

Following a brief examination, the doctor concurred that Dad may have suffered a stroke, but he couldn't be sure. He prescribed more testing. Dad would need to be admitted again.

Dad's estimated short hospital stay turned into a nine-day coast down a slippery and dangerous slope. Every test came back inconclusive. Every test led his team of doctors to run even more tests. The doctors kept insisting that Dad's case was very complex, but they were confident that they could get to the source of his medical problem.

Dad was becoming very depressed and more detached from reality with each additional day in the hospital. Nothing could rouse or uplift him, not even visits from his grandchildren and great grandchildren – formerly the absolute panacea for anything that ailed my father.

We knew that Dad suffered from Shy-Drager Syndrome. Shy-Drager is a multiple-system atrophy with autonomic failure, a progressive disorder of the central and autonomic nervous systems. The disorder is characterized by postural hypotension – an excessive drop in blood pressure which causes dizziness or momentary blackouts upon standing or sitting up. One type of Shy-Drager, the cerebellar type, may include problems such as loss of balance and the tendency to fall. Shy-Drager usually ends in death seven to ten years after the onset of symptoms. (*National Institute of Neurological Disorders and Stroke*).

This diagnosis, obtained just weeks before Mom died, completely cracked the mysterious code surrounding the frequent falling episodes that Dad had suffered for nearly eighteen months straight a few years prior. Nearly thirty-five years earlier he had been diagnosed with Alzheimer's Disease, but that diagnosis had now been replaced with the Shy-Drager opinion. The doctors treating and testing Dad at this moment knew of the diagnosis but were not convinced that it was the acute problem. He wasn't falling, he wasn't dizzy, and his blood pressure was not erratic; it was high and staying that way. They continued testing.

By now, Shy-Drager had completely robbed Dad of his hearing. This man who loved to talk, socialize, and who enjoyed music so much was now deaf. His world of silence only drove him further and further into complete despair. We communicated with him via an erasable communication board, a sort of "etch-a-sketch" or "mini-whiteboard," but with a stylus for writing. Visitors would write a brief question or comment and then hand the board to Dad. He would then verbalize his answer or simply write "yes" or "no" on the board. The questions and "conversations" continued, but soon there were no responses coming from Dad. He would just look at the board with a very sad and empty stare.

Dad was subjected to a daily battery of tests. The results were always the same – inconclusive. The daily walks down the halls of the hospital were becoming fewer and fewer as he refused to leave his room. The inactivity caused Dad to weaken to the point where he only had strength enough to move to the recliner situated next to his bed.

Finally, the hospital environment and the lack of social contact and outside stimulation broke Dad's spirit. He was refusing to get out of bed and his food intake was steadily decreasing. We feared that if he did not get out of the hospital and back to his familiar environment he would reach a point of no return.

As Dad's health declined, Sandie and I became more aggressive with his specialists. Why the decline? How many more tests do you think you need to run? Why is blood now suddenly coming from his catheter? Why isn't he receiving addition physical therapy? Why? Why? Why? Enter a new player onto the stage of my emotions – I was getting scared. I did not want to lose my dad and I was beginning to fear the worst. Dad was responding to nothing and to no one. Not even his grandchildren could spark his interest to speak, go for hallway strolls, eat . . . nothing. I realized very plainly that this was a place I had been before. I did not want to – I could not – go back there.

Over the nine days, Sandie and I met and talked with doctors and specialists, too numerous to recall. Occasionally we would get a theory, an educated guess, or a hypothesis regarding Dad's condition, diagnosis or prognosis. But, for the most part, we got more questions than answers. We came to believe that there were just too many physicians involved (that too many cooks in the soup theory) who were not even communicating with each other, much less the two of us. It got to the point that the medical team seemed annoyed with us because we never stopped asking questions.

Note to caregivers: Annoy the physicians! Do not be afraid to ask questions. You have every right to know what is taking place and physicians have a responsibility to tell you what they know. That said, remember the following as well: Physicians – even the best ones – might not have the answers, plain and simple. Patience, give and take, and reasonable expectations are helpful components in the patient/caregiver/physician relationship. As frustrated as you are, the physician who doesn't know the answer could be equally or more frustrated because s/he cannot help you the way they truly want to. A physician worth his/her salt will be very frustrated, even agitated, when s/he cannot provide the care that your loved one deserves.

Finally, knowing nothing more nine days later than we knew before, we asked Dad's general practitioner to have him discharged. The day before we planned Dad's escape back to the environment he knew and loved, we were greeted by a hospital social worker.

"We have spoken to your dad's specialists and therapists," she said. "They do not feel that he is strong enough to go home unless you can provide twenty-four hour care. They are suggesting that he be transferred to a facility for short term rehabilitation to strengthen his legs."

Instantly, my mind and my spirit raced again to that place we'd been before. My anger at the situation and suggestion, not that poor social worker, turned quickly to sarcasm.

"That's amazing!" I blurted. "He's only gotten weaker since he was admitted here and now you're suggestion a nursing home? Let's just put him in another place completely unfamiliar to him – Yes, that should do the trick!"

I don't know if the social worker really meant what she said next, or if she was just giving me a dose of my own bitter, sarcastic medicine.

"You seem upset. Getting upset is not going to help your father. I'm sorry, but the fact is that your dad's insurance wants him to be discharged tomorrow. Let's take a break and I'll come back later . . . once you're feeling a little better."

Not even a spoonful of sugar was going to help this medicine go down.

"Don't patronize me! You bet I'm upset! I'll discuss this with my sister and I'll let you know what our decision is as soon as possible."

That afternoon Sandie and I had a serious heart to heart conversation. If Dad was going to return home with her, he would certainly need one-on-one and nearly twenty-four hour care. Sandie said several times, "Tom it's all about Dad's dignity. He lets me do allot for him, but I don't know how far he would allow me to go with his personal needs. He's going to need to be lifted and I am physically unable to do that. The only way we could bring him home would be for all of us to move in together and that's not even in the realm of possibility."

Sandie and I both worked, and leaving our jobs was simply not a viable option for either of us. Dad did not have long-term care insurance and his Medicaid Waiver coverage would only afford him a few hours of home care a day. Collectively we could not afford to hire someone on a private pay basis. We felt helpless and deprived of all alternative options. The long term care facility seemed to be our only hope for rehabilitation and our last hope for a chance at a homecoming.

As always, we adopted a positive outlook and did our best to put the same kind of spin on this ordeal. Surely, we thought, Dad would only need a week or two before he would be back on his feet and able to return to Sandie's and to daycare.

So, once again, we called Kathy at the same long term care facility where Mom had been. For a second time she worked her magic. Dad was transferred the next morning.

Deaf But Not Dumb

As we prepared Dad for his transfer, he actually had a look of relief on his face. As we packed his clothes and personal items, he would simply point to a drawer, his way of reminding us to check one more time to ensure that nothing would be left behind. He was ready to get out of the hospital and did not want to come back for any reason.

We had explained to Dad that he was going to go to "Kathy's place" for a few weeks of rehabilitation. The harder he worked, the sooner he could go back to Sandie's. He loved Kathy and had fond memories of her at past social, church and family events. We had hoped that this familiarity would make for a smooth transition and a successful rehabilitation. It had entered our minds that Dad would not fully understand where he was going. The fact is, he did know. We would learn that soon enough. But we learned an even sadder truth equally soon. He knew where he was going, alright, but he didn't particularly care.

Upon arriving at the facility, Dad started therapy and his appetite seemed to be improving slightly. But only three days into his stay, he had the revelation that we thought he might have, but secretly hoped he wouldn't. By now, he wasn't speaking aloud. He only whispered. In that same hushed tone he asked, "Isn't this where Mom was at?"

"Yes," Sandie wrote onto the whiteboard.

Once again, the "experts" score a big fat zero when this caregiving thing hits home. We had completely underestimated Dad's ability to comprehend or to remember the events that had taken place some fourteen months prior. Why would we think he could? After all, here was a man who could remember and retell, in living color, stories of his childhood or his days in the military sixty years ago, but couldn't begin to tell you what took place in his world just sixty minutes ago! I wondered if "the great pretender" was up to his old tricks again.

As a caregiver, and as a son, I had mistaken Dad's silence for confusion. I was sure, arrogantly so, I know now, that he would be so confused that he would just "give in," get with the program and work toward recovery. Because his world had fallen silent, because he rarely spoke, I gave him no credit for his strong will and determination. Only he wasn't at all determined to do what we wanted him to do. He was determined to do what he wanted to do. Just because a person suffers several disabilities does not mean that s/he has no ability. What we discovered all too soon in this final leg of the journey is that Dad must have been taking copious notes during Mom's stay here. Just as we had all learned so much from Mom while she lived, Dad too had learned one very important lesson from her – how to die. Mind you, there was a constant stream of visitors to the facility to see him – children, grandchildren, other friends and family – but in his silent world, when he was all alone, Dad had all the time in the world to replay the events of fourteen months prior.

On the fourth day of his stay, Dad began to refuse his daily medications. He was unresponsive to the therapists who worked so hard to encourage him to walk. Food trays were left pristine on his bed table and any effort on our part to entice him to take a bite was met with the stubbornness of a two year old refusing to eat his peas. Sandie tried everything to get Dad to eat, but not even the daughter whom he idolized could get one morsel past his firmly closed lips.

On those sun drenched days of autumn, I would wheel Dad onto the beautiful front porch that surrounded the facility. My whiteboard conversations fell on literal deaf ears and a figuratively dead spirit.

"Look at the leaves changing color," I cajoled.

No response, no smile, no Dad.

"Are you warm enough? Do you want me to take you for a walk? How about we get in the car and go for a ride?"

My questions were greeted by the same blank stare that landed him here in the first place.

After a week of this torture, I decided to try the "bad cop" routine. After all, it had been so successful when Sandie tried it with Mom! Right. I had a better chance of getting Dad to run the Boston Marathon, but what the heck. Maybe I could bully him into eating his peas. Doesn't that work with two year olds?

"You know, Dad, Mom decided to leave us and now you're doing the same thing. Does it matter to you that I'm not ready to lose both of my parents? Do you want me, and Sandie and David to be orphans? Is that what you want? You have got to snap out of this, and I mean *now!*"

Somehow I must have thought that at least the look of terror on my face as I spoke would permeate the deafness and he would come to his senses. I am grateful to this day that it didn't. I meant what I said – I was not ready for Dad to leave us. But had he heard what I said and, even more, how I said it, I would have truly been ashamed of how I had just spoken to my father. I was ashamed enough and he hadn't even heard me. This gentle, loving creature who never raised his own voice would have left this earth wondering if his son had learned a damn thing from him his entire life.

Okay, terror hadn't worked. Let's try sadness. I'll show him how sad I am. He hates when I'm sad. He hates when any of us is sad. He despises sadness. Sadness should do it. I'm sad, Dad! Do you hear me? I'm sad . . . incredibly and uncontrollably sad. Not working. No response. Damnit, Dad! If I just hold you . . . and put my head on your shoulder . . . and cry like a baby . . . will you come back? Will you stay? Please . . . ?

I *said* none of this. I *was* and I *did* every bit of it.

I don't know that there had been a sadder moment in my life than the day of that visit. God willing, there will be none sadder to follow. I don't think I could take it.

Our family had not yet fully recovered from Mom's death, so we certainly weren't ready to say goodbye to the matriarch's widower. But the course Dad had set himself upon was indeed a place we'd been before, and it became daily more apparent that Dad wanted one thing – to go to a place he hadn't been before.

When Will I Ever Learn?

(Editorial note: Factoring in step and half siblings, my father was one of twenty three children growing up on that farm! The confusion that must have reigned in such a setting is the only explanation I can offer for Dad's given birth name – "Pearl." Family lore has it that his mother had both a boy's and a girl's name in reserve awaiting his birth. When he finally arrived, she couldn't decide, so she assigned both. I prefer my "mass confusion" theory over the idea that any mother would consciously do that to her son! It's helped me to forgive "Grandma Maggie" over the years. His siblings and countless nieces and nephews, until the day he died, called Dad "PE" – short for Pearl Edward. No others ever called him that. Dad actually registered to the military as simply "Edward P. Clark" to avoid any embarrassment. I don't imagine one could ever get away with such deception today. It was always fascinating when this bit of trivia would come up over the years. Children, grandchildren, cousins and in-laws were always stunned at the revelation. While everyone agreed that the name fit him as it related to his preciousness, they were equally happy to continue referring to him as "Grandpa" or "Clark." So, imagine that. My father, the trailblazer – He had a name like "Pearl" decades before Johnny Cash had "A Boy Named Sue!")

Family visits to see Dad had become as silent as the world in which he was confined. His grandchildren would enter the room, give him a kiss, and take their seat alongside the bed. They didn't want to disturb his sleep which, by now, consumed nearly twenty hours of his day. He would be aroused by staff to eat (sit upright and stare at his food or into space) or wheeled down to the common room to socialize with the other residents (sit upright and stare at *them* and into space). By now, Sandie and I had even quit talking (no small miracle to anyone who knows us!).

We sat in complete silence, too sad to speak and realizing the folly of it all anyway. As Dad would always say, "You know, honey, I don't hear so good no more."

No kidding, Dad . . . no kidding.

During one such "visit with myself" and the beautiful man in the bed, my mind started to wander. It behooved me, I thought, to be practical and to start "planning ahead." What would our family look like without Dad – without Grandpa? Who would carry on in his place? There was no "PIT" (Patriarch In Training) in this year's budget, nor was there ever a discussion regarding proper succession to the throne. I thought that David and I should call William and Harry, The Princes of Wales, to ask them how this whole blasted thing works. Who would tell the stories of Dad's growing up on the farm or his adventures serving his country as a Medic in World War II? Would we remember how to stack split wood properly? Would he leave us without the recipe for his mother's angel-wing biscuits? I felt the pressure of the final exam coming on, and me? I had forgotten to cram.

I left that place quickly. I didn't like that place very much so I brought myself back to Dad's room. And there we sat . . . in the silence.

On my way home from work on the evening of November 7th, I called Sandie from the car.

"What kind of day did Dad have?" I asked.

"No change," she replied. "Melissa just left and said she couldn't get him to wake up."

"I'm going to stop on my way home. I'll call you after I leave."

I arrived to visit with Dad at 6:00 p.m. and found him just as Melissa had described to Sandie. Although I thought Dad's breathing was a little shallow, he appeared to be in a peaceful sleep. I gave him a kiss on the cheek and he opened his eyes. I smiled and said, "Well, hi there Sleeping Beauty. Are you going to stay awake and visit?"

Of course, Dad couldn't hear a word I was saying and I didn't even think he would be alert enough to read anything that I might write on the whiteboard. He knew from my smile, though, that I was glad to see him.

As I stood above him holding his hand, he suddenly began to whisper. I was in near shock as he hadn't even attempted to verbally communicate in days. I lowered my ear to his mouth.

"I want to go home," he barely got out in a winded whisper.

"You want to go to Sandie's?" I frantically wrote on the whiteboard.

Dad shook his head after reading it and repeated, "I want to go home."

"With me? You want to come live with Steve and me?"

"No . . . home . . . to Mom."

My mouth fell open and my eyes widened. Could I have heard him correctly? Was he telling me he wanted to go to see Mom? Indeed, he was. I can't say that his longing surprised me. But to hear him actually say it threw my emotions into a complete tail spin that came to rest at anger. And in yet a second display of everything I hadn't learned from the man in the bed, I launched into full scold.

"Fine, Dad! You just go right ahead and give up – just like Mom! That's fine. If you want to leave us, you just go right ahead, but you know what? I'm going home! I'm not sticking around to watch!"

Once again, I hoped for a miracle – my miracle. Never mind him. This has nothing to do with him. It's all about me! Having completed the shortest sermon of my ordained life, spoken to a congregation of one who couldn't hear it anyway, I started out of the room. Having felt that the "two cents" I had just offered was rather a paltry sum, I turned to offer more. Dad was staring at me. Not into space – at me. He looked like a child. He wore a pathetic frown and his crystal blue eyes were fixed on mine, the exact replica of his own. Usually at no loss for words, I could think of only two that would free me from this most uncomfortable moment.

"Good night!"

As I tried to start my car, my entire body began to shake and tears rolled down my face. They quickly turned into an all out sob.

What am I doing? The caregiver in me knows that this is how it all ends. No one lives forever. Dad had paid his taxes, and now the other "sure thing in life" was just around the corner. Pull yourself together, Tom. But it wasn't the caregiver who was sobbing. It was Pearl Edward Clark's son, Thomas Edward, who sat in that car weeping and who had just left his father, probably for the last time, with nothing kinder to say than "Good night."

I remained in the darkness of the parking lot praying and pondering. Now calming somewhat, my spirit revealed to me the same obvious truth it had revealed fourteen months earlier. Dad was looking for my permission to go and be with Mom. They had been married for over fifty-seven years and he missed her more than words on a page can ever express. He wasn't saying that he didn't love me, Sandie, David, his grandchildren, his life. He was simply saying that he loved no one more than his wife and he simply could not live without her. I knew what I needed to do. And that little voice called "conscience" wasn't going to leave me alone until I did.

I got out of my car and rushed back into the building and into Dad's room. He was still awake, still staring at the doorway. I have no doubt in my mind that he absolutely knew that I would be back. He knew that the son he had raised was so much better than "Good night."

I stood next to him and took firm hold of his hand. I tried my best to smile. I picked up the whiteboard and began to write.

"Dad, I'm sorry I was so mean. You have been the best dad in the world. I love you!"

His blue eyes read the board, slowly, one word at a time.

"I know you want to be with Mom. I came back to tell you that it's okay."

More reading followed by a slight nod. And then I concluded this much more gentle exchange.

"Tell Mom I said hi and I send my love. And tell her she better be nice to you or she's in big trouble when I get up there!"

If blue eyes can smile, I'm pretty sure they did that night. Dad's expression softened. I knew he understood because he closed his eyes and fell fast asleep. I stood waiting to make sure he wasn't going to wake up. I didn't want him to open his eyes to an empty room.

I began to reflect. Did he understand my apology? More importantly, did he accept it? Does he know that it's really okay to leave? Did he feel my sincerity when I wrote that I loved him? Within moments a peace came over me. All of the tension in my body, the pain in my back from hunching over the bed, the pain in my head that crying guarantees, all of it was gone. The answer to all of my questions was a resounding "yes." I turned to leave. From the doorway, I turned around to take one more look at him. I knew that everything was going to be alright.

The Homecoming

As I walked into our home Steve was on the phone. I heard him say to the caller, "He just got home."

Hanging up, he then turned to greet me. He knew that I had been to see Dad. He held me tightly. I was sure that he was going to tell me that Dad was gone. Instead, he spoke softly and said, "Honey, that was Sandie. The nursing home just called her and told her that the family needs to get there as soon as possible. Dad is getting ready to leave us."

Steve grabbed his coat and we prepared for what would be a very quiet ride back to the nursing home. The silence was broken only occasionally by a sniffle from me or an "Are you alright?" from Steve. I did my best to reassure him that I was fine, but he knew the truth. Lovingly, he simply allowed the much needed silence.

As we entered the nursing home I told Steve that it was important for me to stay as calm as possible. I didn't want to add to my family's sadness. Steve replied, "Okay, the silence was better! Why would you say something like that? Everyone is sad and you're allowed to be sad too."

His rebuke reminded me just how much like my mother I really was, or at least wanted to be. Always in control . . . always the pillar . . . always the voice of certainty and reassurance, ignoring myself for the sake of others. Right. I was a mess and, as far as Steve was concerned, that was just fine.

As we walked into the room, it was crowded with Sandie and Bill, Shawn, Stacey, Melissa and Kevin. There was an almost audible sound of relief that we had arrived. My family viewed Sandie and me as the "pillars" in times like these. What a burden that would be on this night.

Sandie was applying a cool wash cloth to Dad's forehead. I embraced her with the tightest hug I had ever given my sister. I leaned over and kissed Dad.

"Dad, it's okay. Remember, you can go see Mom. Just rest. We'll be fine."

Steve was on the other side of Dad's bed holding his hand. He placed a long kiss on Dad's forehead.

"Dad, I love you. It's okay . . . it's okay."

Tears filled his eyes as he reached across the bed for Sandie's hand.

"I love you, Sister."

"I love you too, Brother."

We remained at vigil for a few more hours. At just after midnight on November 8th, Dad quietly left us to be with his beloved wife. Even in death, the southern gentleman he always was came shining through. No fuss, no grandstanding. He just stopped breathing.

"Uncle Tom?" Shawn asked through tear-filled eyes.

"Grandpa's gone," I said softly, calmly, and with as much quiet joy as I could muster.

Bill left the room immediately to find the nurse. Those present gathered into a circle to console one another. Sandie and I just stood over the lifeless body of the man we called "Daddy" and said a prayer of thanksgiving for everything he had taught us and a prayer for his safe journey home.

The nurse arrived and did what a nurse does. No blood pressure, no heart beat, no respiration. She turned to us and spoke with great compassion, "Your dad is with your mom. And that's where he wants to be. You can be sad for you, but don't be sad for him. He was a wonderful man. It was my honor to have been able to take care of him in his last days. You spend as much time as you want with him. Let me know when you're ready to leave. I'll be at my desk."

The room had grown so quiet that it hurt my ears. Sandie broke the silence by announcing her intention to wait until sunrise to call David.

"No sense waking him," she surmised.

We all agreed. We remained in the room for about an hour when it was clear that everyone needed to go home and get some rest. As we prepared to leave, I glanced around the room to find that another circle had spontaneously formed around Dad's bed. It was like we were making one last attempt to prevent his spirit from leaving us. We knew better, of course, but it was worth a try.

We knew from whence our strength had come these past fourteen months. We joined hands. Sandie placed her hand on Dad's right shoulder and I placed mine on his left. This one last time, Dad took his place at the head of the family as the circle closed. We endeavored to thank the giver of our strength, the one who is far greater and more powerful than the sorrow we were feeling, for the blessing of this night.

"Lord, you have received Dad home. We know his reunion with you and Mom is wonderful. You have received one of your very best back home. We're going to need your help in the days, weeks and months to come. Please help us. Amen."

It was after 2:00 a.m. and it was time to go. Most of us had worked a full day and we needed some rest. As we slowly filed from the room, Steve turned and paused to look at Dad's door.

"Sandie, can I have this?" he asked.

It was a sign with Dad's name on it. It was made of orange and yellow construction paper decorated with pumpkin and turkey stickers and Dad's name written in glitter. I'm sure it had been created for the approaching Thanksgiving holiday by some young volunteers who wished to brighten up an otherwise sad place. Sandie smiled and put her hand on Steve's shoulder.

"Sure, Brother. You can take it."

Steve gingerly peeled it from the tape that secured it to the door. First one corner, then the next, so careful not to disfigure the piece of art that had marked the entrance to the room of a saint.

We Know What You're Going Through . . . Really, We Do

After a very restless night, Steve and I met Sandie and Bill at the funeral home. Thankfully, Mom had completed all of Dad's arrangements at the same time she had made her own. We basically needed to fill in the blanks with the names of new great-grandchildren and other information for his obituary, and our task was complete.

The remainder of that day was quiet and somber as Steve and I moved about our home trying our best to have a normal day. Steve retreated to our home office to do some busywork, and I did what Mom would have done – I began to clean. With the steady whir of the vacuum cleaner, the scent of Clorox bleach and the rhythmic beat of the washer, I was moving in high gear. I was on a mission to keep my mind occupied.

As I ascended the basement stairs, Steve stood at the top with a warm and humorous smile across his face.

"What?" I asked, as we stood face to face in the kitchen.

"Nothing, honey. You're just like your Mom," he teased.

"Well you know, someone might stop over and I don't want them to see the house a mess," I defended.

"When has our home ever been a mess? I'm sure that anyone who comes here will immediately run to the basement to see if there are any dirty clothes in the basket!" he chuckled.

"Well, you know what I mean."

From there I headed straight for the second floor bathroom, Clorox in tow. I would never admit it verbally, but Steve was absolutely right. I had become my mother! Frankly, if I thought I had the time, I would have disassembled the bed frames and made an all out search for dust bunnies lurking beneath them.

At around 7:00 p.m., our back door opened and we heard, "Hello, is anybody home?"

"Come on in," I shouted.

As Steve and I made our way through the living room to greet our unexpected guests, I looked at him and quipped, "See? Aren't you glad that I cleaned today?"

He just laughed.

"Absolutely, honey."

Our closest and dearest circle of friends (actually, they are far more like family than friends) filed in. It was like a parade of supporters coming to a political rally. As the procession continued through the back door each had hands full of gifts to nourish the body. Amy and Butch bore gifts of wine and beer (yes, I said nourish!), Judy, Kandy, and their daughter, Klara, presented a meat and cheese tray, and Alice and Karla handed us wonderful desserts and a fruit tray.

"We thought you might need some company . . . not to mention a glass or two of wine!" Amy laughed.

During the nearly two years of caregiving, Steve and I had made a conscious effort to avoid isolation and the neglect of our circle of friends. They serve to keep us grounded in the truth that, regardless of what is going on in one's life, the world goes on. They had kept our emotional and spiritual wells full when they would become dangerously depleted. Throughout the many years of our friendships, they have served as our lifelines when life came hard at us and tried to throw us off course.

Caregivers can become so involved and entrenched in their day to day efforts that, without realizing it, they cut the very ties that can sustain them. When this happens, caregivers often feel abandoned or forgotten. Only later do they realize that it was *they* who walked away. Good friends forgive such behavior, of course, because they truly love you and try to understand what you were going through. But why wait until the journey is through? Caregivers, keep your ties with your close friends. Maintaining those relationships is so important to your own well being. Don't go it alone – You get no awards at the end for being "brave" and going solo! You might get one for being a misguided martyr, but certainly not one for your bravery. There is absolutely no justification that I can think of for taking this journey alone when you have good friends who are willing to travel with you. Spending time with these people, when you are able, will give you the strength and energy you need when you are immersed in caregiving and not able to be with them.

We all took our seats in the living room, "adult tasty beverage" in hand, and settled in to reminisce. No sooner had we done so than Karla announced, "Well, I'm hungry! You don't think we brought all of this food just for you guys, do you?"

We all roared! It was good to hear our home filled with laughter again after such a dismal past few days. As Karla approached the hastily arranged buffet at our dining room table, Steve, Judy and Butch followed in hot pursuit. Our individual and collective relationships work well that way. Alice, Amy, Kandy and I love to cook and our spouses love to eat! The four cooks in our group have a motto: We eat because we have to. They eat because they love to. Many a wonderful evening has been spent around a dining room table at one of our homes.

"How are you doing Tom?" Alice asked in a concerned and loving tone.

Raising the glass of wine to my lips, I said, "I'm okay. I just can't believe that he's gone."

I took a sip of the wine and displayed for all present just how "okay" I was. I broke into tears again and tried to catch my breath and regain my composure. I don't know what it is about that Alice, but I avoid going to sad movies with her. We would undoubtedly be asked to leave. Alice, the consummate crier, reached for her purse to retrieve a tissue from her never ending supply. Handing me a tissue and keeping several for herself she said,

"Oh Tom, your Dad was such a good man. It's okay to miss him."

Amy, second only to Alice in tear duct prowess, had also retrieved a tissue previously hidden somewhere on her person. To this day I have no idea where it came from. It was like "Spiderman's" web – where does it come from? Who knows? It's just there. Having wiped her eyes, she began to share a story in hopes of lifting the spirits in the room.

"Do you remember the night we all came over for the bonfire while your dad was visiting you guys? Butchie and I showed up after a work event we had to go to. I had stupidly eaten strawberries and was covered with hives? Your dad was so concerned. The next day in church, he sought me out to make sure I was feeling better. What a sweetheart of a man he was."

The evening continued on just like that. Stories and memories one after the other. A true trip down memory lane. I've often said that if tears cleanse the soul, then the eight of us had souls fit for their reward after that night of fellowship. The laughter and the tears brought instant healing to our hurting hearts, a soothing balm for our suffering. In the back of my mind I knew that Dad would have enjoyed every minute of our being together. He loved our friends as much as they loved him because he always knew how much they meant to us.

Caregivers, I can't say this enough. That night was made possible because those friends truly knew and came to love my dad and my mom. We never stopped involving that close circle of friends in our caregiving journey. Sometimes, I suspect, they probably wished we hadn't! But we did, and we have no regrets. If a friend approaches you at the end of the journey – at calling hours, for instance – and says to you, "I know what you're going through," and your internal reaction is something like, "You can't possibly know what I'm going through," then I would have this question for you. Why *don't* they know? Perhaps you should have told them.

And if you are one who lives with that regret now, don't worry. You'll get another chance. You probably haven't "caregiven" for the last time. Life is great that way. You almost always get a second chance.

The Great Pumpkin!

Steve and I left the house early for Dad's calling hours. We wanted to make sure everything was ready before the rest of our family and friends arrived. I'm not big on surprises and did not want any awaiting me at the church where calling was to be held.

As we walked into the narthex, we could once again smell the beautiful flowers that adorned the area, just like fourteen months prior. We had asked that, in lieu of flowers, memorial gifts be given to the church. To our amazement, most who sent flowers also made the requested gift.

As I moved around the room looking at the cards that were displayed on the arrangements, I eventually made my way to the casket that held Dad's remains. I stopped. I just stood and stared, as if frozen in time and place. Steve read my body language from across the room and asked, "Honey, what's wrong?"

"Oh my God, he's orange! Dad looks orange. Steven, come over here!

Don't you think he looks orange?" I bantered on.

As we both intently stared at Dad, we concurred that he indeed looked orange. And not just pale, like peach. This was orange. No, this was *Crayola* orange – the kind you find in the 64-pack, with the nifty sharpener, orange!

My heart nearly stopped as I began to imagine my sister's reaction. "Steve, go get someone from the funeral home . . . quick!"

Steve literally ran to the funeral staff who had gathered in the parking lot awaiting callers. He went to the closest one he could find.

"Hurry! My father-in-law is orange. If you don't want another funeral here today, someone has got to fix this immediately!"

The next thing I heard was the sound of feet running up the tiled hallway leading to the narthex. As I stood motionless in front of the casket, the funeral directors and Steve surrounded me.

"He does look orange," someone said.

"Too much makeup and probably not the best choice of color," another chimed in.

My patience was wearing thin. I turned and said, in my "outside" voice, "Listen, guys, you have approximately five minutes before my sister gets here. If she sees that you have turned our dad into the "Great Pumpkin," you may be the next one lying in state in this narthex! Now, what can we do to fix this and fix it quickly?"

Judging by the stunned looks on their faces, I believe they truly feared Sandie's arrival. As they stood looking at Dad and then at one another, I loudly asked again, "What are you going to do? You've got to do something!"

Panic had entered my voice. I think that even I was fearful of Sandie's arrival by this time.

"You know," said one of the directors to the others and to me. "We thought that the natural light from the wall of windows behind the casket would have added a nice touch, but I think we need to get the lamps."

One by one they agreed and began to congratulate the young "Einstein" among them for his brilliant suggestion.

As an ordained pastor I have been to or presided over literally hundreds of funerals. At every single one, a raised lamp is placed at the head of the casket, and often one at the foot as well. It absolutely never occurred to me that it was there for any other reason than to create some ambience by casting some soft light. I had no idea it was actually stage lighting for the show! I couldn't believe that it hadn't occurred to me.

I looked back at the funeral directors and asked quickly, "So where are these lamps?"

"They're at the funeral home. We'll leave right now. It will only take about ten minutes for us to get back. We should have them in place before your sister gets here."

"Great . . . go, go, go!" I ordered.

Again the sound of grown men running from the narthex and down the hall echoed throughout the building. I grabbed both of Steve's arms and said in utter desperation, "We have got to keep Sandie out of the narthex until they get back with those lamps. If she sees Dad looking like this she'll freak! I don't think either one of us wants to see that. You've got to help me!"

Poor Steve. He had never seen me – or anyone, for that matter – about to have a nervous breakdown.

"So, how do you suppose we keep Sandie out of here until they get back?" he asked. "You know she'll be here any minute. That girl would show up on time for her own execution!"

"That's not an answer! That's what I'm asking you! HELP! She'll be here any minute!"

Steve swallowed and calmly asked, "Uh . . . could you let go of my arms? You're hurting me."

Immediately, he came up with a plan.

"I'll wait for Bill and Sandie in the parking lot. I'll stall them with meaningless but charming conversation."

His eyes sought my approval.

"Brilliant," I replied. "You can do that. You have meaningless conversations all the time – er . . . I mean, charming conversations . . . brilliant but charm . . . I mean, meaningless . . . Whatever! Just go! I'll wait right here!"

Steve ran feverishly down the hall. For my part, I prayed silently.

Just as I was finishing my plea I heard voices coming up the hallway. I had hoped it was the funeral directors returning with the lamps. But I recognized these voices. It was Sandie, Bill and Steve! He had failed in his mission. Not only was I now an orphan, but I was about to be cured of my "middle child syndrome" by virtue of my sister dropping dead to the floor! Panic ensued and I ran to greet them in the hallway.

"Oh, hi!" I exclaimed. "Everything is fine. Wait until you see the flowers. The narthex looks great! Are David and Wanda on their way? When do you think the kids will be getting here?"

Talk about meaningless and charming. I had definitely succeeded where Steven had failed.

The three of them just stood there looking at me. They must have thought I was having that nervous breakdown. Ten seconds of silence passed before my sister put her arms around me and drew me closer to her.

"Tom, are you alright?" she asked. "Why are you sweating? Do they have the heat set too high, honey? I'll go check."

"NO! It's fine. You know, why don't we just wait out here for David and the kids to arrive? Don't you think it would be nice for us all to go in and see Dad together? I do. What a great family thing to do!"

I nervously smiled. Sandie and Bill slowly turned and looked at Steve inquisitively. Again Steve swallowed. He quickly concocted a response,

"Tom's right. Nothing was more important to Dad than family."

"Are you guys okay?" Sandie asked again.

"Sure! We're fine!" I smiled.

"Well, if you want to wait for the rest of the family to arrive, go right ahead. I'm going into the narthex," she announced with determination.

"Alright, alright! There's a slight issue," I reluctantly confessed. "Not to worry, though. The guys from the funeral home have assured me that they can take care of the problem."

"Problem? There's a problem?"

Sandie's voice raised at least two octaves.

"It's not that big of a deal," I tried to convince.

Sandie had had enough of my stalling tactics.

"I'll be the judge of that."

She made her way quickly past Steve and me and descended upon the Great Pumpkin's patch!

I followed closely on Sandie's heels as she approached the casket. Would I have to catch her when she passed out or would her knees simply buckle sending her in a heap onto the floor? Stopping at least three feet away she stated aloud what she had just laid eyes on.

"He's orange! They painted Daddy orange! My God, Tom, he looked better the night he died! He's orange!"

"Well, actually, Steve and I discussed this just before you got here and we thought he looks more . . . uh . . . peach. Yea, it's more peach than orange."

I tried desperately to get her to agree.

"Tom, Daddy is freakin' orange!"

Oh my God! My sister just said "freakin!" I've never heard my sister say that before. I've never heard anything even close to that cross her lips. Enough about Dad! My sister said "freakin!" Now I knew there was going to be trouble. All I could do was look at Dad and concede, "Yep . . . he's orange, alright. He looks like a great big pumpkin."

The room was silent for a few seconds. Just as I thought that the initial shock and anger had died down, Sandie started again.

"If we don't do something to fix this and our family sees Dad looking like a Halloween leftover, we will be holding a mass funeral for the entire Clark family here tomorrow!"

"It will be alright," I assured her. "The funeral home knows how to fix it."

Sarcastically, she responded, "What are they going to do? Wash his face? Maybe spray him with a contrasting color? What do you think of GREEEEN?"

"No, they're bringing lamps."

"Lamps?"

"Uh . . . yea . . . the guys from the funeral home forgot to bring them when they brought Daddy to the church. They should be back with two magnificent lamps at any moment. Some day we'll look back at all of this and laugh. Won't we? Er . . . uh . . . Aren't the flowers beautiful?"

Okay, sometimes humor works. And sometimes it just doesn't. This was one of those "doesn'ts." Just as I thought the time had arrived for me to call the EMS – not for my sister, but for me – the men returned from the funeral home with two floor lamps.

"Here we are," said one of the directors. "This will fix it. It's the lighting in this room. Too much outside light and these bright fluorescents. It sure does make our work look bad."

I had never seen my sister inflict bodily harm on so much as a flea. I thought tonight might be the night.

"Plug those in," she scolded, "and I'll let you know if it's fixed! You made my father orange. And if he stays orange we're going to have real trouble here!"

It's amazing how even the most gentle of creatures has the capability to turn violent over, say, painting her father orange. This was a sight. My heart broke for Sandie because this was so unlike her. She loathes acting this way, but the matter was simply out of her emotional control. She continued her orders to the men in the suits.

"Gentlemen, don't just stand there. Put the lamps where you think they should go."

I believe in trusting folks until something happens that would cause me to distrust. Still, I had full faith in these three men to fix the problem. But I also believe in being prepared with a "Plan B." So, just in case their lamp idea turned out to be a bust, Steve and I had positioned ourselves between Sandie and the funeral staff.

Now came the big moment. The lamps had been plugged in and the directors were about to turn them on. Not a sound could be heard. No one moved. I considered postponing or stopping my breathing altogether.

I heard the lamps click on, but I was afraid to open my eyes. Coward that I am, I waited for Sandie to look first. How did I know that she didn't have her eyes closed waiting for me? I waited. Still silent. I waited some more. Then, finally, an audible "Ahhh" filled the room. I could breathe again. I opened my eyes and everyone was nodding in agreement that all was well. The Great Pumpkin was earthtones once again.

Who Was Rosie John?

The following is the eulogy written and delivered by my partner,
Steven Begert-Clark, at my father's funeral

When I first became a member of the Clark Clan, I was told of a woman – I supposed she was a woman – named "Rosie John."

"Who is that?" I asked Tom and the boys.

"Oh we don't really know," they replied. "It's just something that Grandpa used to say, maybe when he was mad about something, or maybe even when he was glad to see one of us, surprised to see a relative, stunned at the day's 6:00 news. Oh, 'Rosie John,' he would say, and yet no one ever knew where it came from, who it was, or what it really meant."

The old saying "Ours is not to question why, ours is but to do or die," I believed, did not apply to me. I must know not only why, but how and where, how many and how much, which way and what time, why not and how come.

And so I endeavored to ask Dad, on several occasions, "Dad, who is Rosie John? Where did she come from? Why do you say her name? You don't say it much any more. In fact, (and this is when I asked him only two months ago during his last stay in Warren), I've known you for ten years and I've only heard you say her name once. Tell me of her."

"Well, honey," came his reply. "I don't really know. It's just somethin' I said, I guess. Just somethin' I said."

Then he tipped his head back, chuckling, and asked Tom, "Tom, honey, do you know?"

"No, Daddy, I don't know"

"See, Steve," Dad continued. "I just don't know. Maybe my dad said it, you know, and then maybe I did too."

Head back . . . laughing . . . more laughing. Always, lots and lots of laughing.

Well, Dad, you may not know, but I *must* know. Who is she? Is she beautiful? Is she here? Is she someone who just reminds you of someone else? Is she Stella? Is she nice like you? Does she know that you say her name? Then, I think, is she some "secret code" word between you and Mom that, when uttered at a party, was her cue to start hinting about an early departure?

"Oh, Rosie John!" you would say.

Then, Mom, "Oh, Clark, would you just look at the time? We'd better be going!"

Okay, let's break it down some more. Let's think about *when* you say her name. When? When?

Okay, you're pounding a nail with a hammer. Suddenly, you hit *your* nail with said hammer. Urge to say word or words not likely to be heard in the Sunday sermon but instead, "Rosie John!"

Aha! So, Rosie John is *God* as this is the name most of us would invoke in said "hammer hits nail" scenario! Nah, only God can be God, I think. Rosie can't be God.

Alright, then. A grandchild has spilled milk, walked through the house with muddy feet, broken the vase, or, as grandchildren grew up, brought the girlfriend from the underworld to the Clark family Christmas. And she's there. Rosie John is there because it is better to say *her* name quietly than the offender's name loudly.

And now, life gets tough I mean really tough. Getting older means getting tough. First, you can't drive – too shaky – too dangerous. Rosie John shall be your driver now? Then you can't hear – Doodle pads and post it notes – All alone at the party – Closed caption too fast, gives me headaches. I whisper so you know how *I* feel. Rosie John, the interpreter, perhaps?

Then, try this pill . . . then this pill . . . then this one because it will really work! Blue for blood pressure, yellow for blood count, red for your eyes, pink for your stomach, white for your liver, teal for your ticker, purple for your mood, green for your shakes and one more . . . Orange . . . yes, *that* one for your . . . well, you know. *Doctor* Rosie John, I presume?

Oh wait! I know – I know – She's a nun! Rosie is a nun! She's an Antonine Sister who "don't speak much English, honey, but they're such hard workers, honey, and you can just tell that they love all the people, honey, and it's such hard work, honey." But what are their names, Dad, Sister *who?* Surely they have names!

"No Steve, honey, I think we just call 'em 'Sister.'"

Sister Rosie, then?

Sister *John?*

Sister Rosie *Saint* John?

Oh, I give up! I shall never know her. You're gone now, Dad, and you never told me. I will never see her beauty, I shall never know her love, feel her arms around me, her kiss on my cheek, her laughter in my ear, her "I love you, honey" in my heart. Though I never knew her, I feel like I did and my heart is broken because . . . well . . . already . . . I miss her.

And then it hit me. Like a ton of bricks it hit me. And I knew what to do.

Stand up today and talk of love and laughter, of gentleness and caring, of holiness and happiness, hugs and kisses – Speak of all that *she* was. Yes, that's what I'll do.

Then everyone will know. Yes, everyone will know . . .

That the great Rosie John . . .

Was *you.*

Goodbye, Dad.

Farewell . . . Our "Rosie John."

Epilogue

Ah, yes . . . Our Rosie John had changed his permanent address. We firmly believe that he has been reunited with Mom in a most wonderful and, due to her diligence, clean place! But, oh how we miss him.

December 1ˢᵗ, 2003 arrived and I knew that our traditional family Christmas gathering was right around the corner. And I knew full well that I would be called on to take Dad's normal place and duty at the gathering – that of speaking some words of thanksgiving and wisdom, of Christmas cheer and blessing. I perished the thought. No one could do it like him – I would just as soon our family live in their remembrance of his having done it year after year, so eloquent, so sincere, so "Dad." But Sandie was insistent. She thought, and I concurred, that we needed to "carry on as normal," to make this a good Christmas for the kids and for one another. We couldn't pretend that no one would be thinking about Dad. Bringing it up, talking about it and giving that little speech would be . . . well . . . cathartic, especially for me.

"No thanks, Sister," I retaliated. "Suppose I just sit down some day and write a book about the whole thing! How would that be for catharsis?"

"Funny, Brother – very funny," she replied. "I know you can do this. I won't ask you to do it again, but this first time . . . I think it's so important."

Lady Diana Spencer would have had an easier time putting a halt to the royal wedding than I was having trying to stop this coronation. Me . . . the patriarch . . . It just didn't fit, but I knew what I had to do.

"Oh, alright. I'll do my best. It won't be like Daddy, though, it just won't."

163

Of course it wouldn't be like Dad – there was no one like him. If I had even one-tenth his gentleness, his kindness, his wisdom, and just the tiniest portion of his sincerity, I might come close. But soon I stopped obsessing over what I didn't have and began to celebrate what I did have. Wonderful lasting memories of the most beautiful person I have ever known. Surely, somewhere in all of that would be something to say to and for my family at that gathering. And I knew in my heart, that as I spoke, he would be right there with me. And Mom would be there too.

Yes, it was over now.
The "fat lady" would be singing.
"Rosie John" would be turning pages.
And using my father's simple words, I would say to my family and to both of them . . . my beautiful mom and dad . . .

"Thank you for all that you done for us . . .
Thank you for all that you done."

About the Author

Tom Begert-Clark is a consultant, trainer, motivational specialist, author and humorist. He is a nationally recognized speaker known for his unique, open and humorous approach to business, communications, and life in general.

His experience is vast and varied. He has served as a HUD Service Coordinator and Senior Housing Specialist, Director of an adult daycare center, Eldercare Program Developer, Director of Franchise Support for a national adult day services corporation, and as an Ordained Pastor.

Gathering up his accumulated life skills and his ability to make questionable and everyday stressful situations more palatable, he created his own company, **Even As We Speak**® (www.evenaswespeakonline.com), in 2005.

Tom, a native of Austintown, Ohio now resides in nearby Warren, Ohio with his partner, Steven.

www.ingramcontent.com/pod-product-compliance
Lightning Source LLC
Chambersburg PA
CBHW020916290526
45784CB00002BA/575